Recovering from Sexual Abuse and Incest

A Twelve-Step Guide

Jean Gust
Patricia D. Sweeting

Mills & Sanderson, Publishers
Bedford, MA • 1992

DISCLAIMER

The vignettes, which appear as quoted material in this work, are adapted from the real life experiences of actual abuse survivors. They are used here for the universality of the emotions expressed. All names and other specifics have been fictionalized to insure anonymity and confidentiality.

Published by Mills & Sanderson, Publishers
41 North Road, Suite 201 • Bedford, MA 01730
Copyright © 1992 Jean Gust and Patricia D. Sweeting

Library of Congress Cataloging-in-Publication Data

Gust, Jean, 1948-
    Recovering from sexual abuse and incest: a twelve-step guide / Jean Gust, Patricia D. Sweeting.
        p.   cm.
    Includes resources.
    ISBN 0-938179-32-2 (pbk.): $9.95
    1. Sexual abuse victims--Rehabilitation. 2. Incest victims-
-Rehabilitation. 3. Twelve-step programs. I. Sweeting, Patricia
D., 1943- . II. Title.
RC560.S44G87   1992
616.85'83603--dc20   92-17290
                                                                              CIP

Printed and manufactured by Capital City Press.
Illustrations by Gladys Elaine Kelepouris.
Cover design by Lyrl Ahern.

Printed and Bound in the United States of America

This book is dedicated to all victims of sexual abuse and incest. Too many have not survived; their remains lie in the cemeteries and institutions. To everyone who is still alone and being victimized, we open our hands and hearts and invite you to become a survivor.

In addition, this book is dedicated to all those who have walked beside survivors when we only wanted to be left alone; to those who have helped us up when we fell down and didn't want to get up again; to the people who loved us when we couldn't love ourselves.

The Twelve Steps
for Survivors of Sexual Abuse and Incest

1. We admitted we were powerless over sexual abuse—that our lives had become unmanageable.

2. We came to believe that a Power greater than ourselves could restore us to sanity.

3. We made a decision to turn our will and our lives over to the care of our Higher Power *as we understood that Power.*

4. We made a searching and fearless moral inventory of ourselves.

5. We admitted to our Higher Power, to ourselves and to another human being the exact nature of our wrongs.

6. We were entirely ready to have our Higher Power remove all these defects of character.

7. We humbly asked our Higher Power to remove our shortcomings.

8. We made a list of all persons we had harmed, and became willing to make amends to them all.

9. We made direct amends to such people wherever possible, except when to do so would injure them or others.

10. We continued to take personal inventory, and when we were wrong promptly admitted it.

11. We sought through prayer and meditation to improve our conscious contact with our Higher Power *as we understood that Power,* praying only for knowledge of our Higher Power's will for us and the power to carry that out.

12. Having had a spiritual awakening as the result of these Steps, we tried to carry this message to other sexual abuse survivors, and to practice these principles in all our affairs.

The Twelve Steps
of Alcoholics Anonymous

1. We admitted we were powerless over alcohol—that our lives had become unmanageable.

2. Came to believe that a Power greater than ourselves could restore us to sanity.

3. Made a decision to turn our will and our lives over to the care of God *as we understood Him.*

4. Made a searching and fearless moral inventory of ourselves.

5. Admitted to God, to ourselves, and to another human being the exact nature of our wrongs.

6. Were entirely ready to have God remove all these defects of character.

7. Humbly asked Him to remove our shortcomings.

8. Made a list of all persons we had harmed, and became willing to make amends to them all.

9. Made direct amends to such people wherever possible, except when to do so would injure them or others.

10. Continued to take personal inventory and when we were wrong promptly admitted it.

11. Sought through prayer and meditation to improve our conscious contact with God *as we understood Him,* praying only for knowledge of His will for us and the power to carry that out.

12. Having had a spiritual awakening as the result of these Steps, we tried to carry this message to alcoholics, and to practice these principles in all our affairs.

Foreword

This book is not merely a recapitulation of the Twelve Steps of Alcoholics Anonymous, nor is it just a clearly presented and well thought out explanation of these Steps as they apply to survivors of sexual trauma. It is a labor of love and compassion. It is obvious to the reader that the authors have been living the Twelve Steps and they continue to do so. They have clearly found these Steps to be useful for their own healing. They are like the wounded healers of old who, at a certain point in their own healing, begin to share what they have learned to help others heal as well.

This book is not just for those who already believe in the Twelve Steps. Not everyone is attracted to the Twelve Steps or to the self-help groups which utilize their concepts. In my experience as a clinical psychologist, I have noticed that the individuals who benefit the most from these groups are those who truly *work the program*. That is, they make the Steps a part of themselves and their lives. Some people do not want anyone to tell them how to live their lives. But the Twelve Steps are not rules, they are guidelines which many people have found helpful. Some people think that they cannot relate to the Steps because they seem to be too simplistic. But this is a misreading of them. Though simply stated, they have profound meaning and effect. Some individuals do not feel they can relate to certain people in a particular group. The solution to this is to learn to resolve problems with other members or to attend another group. These individuals might find something in it for themselves if they could be open-minded and try to understand things more deeply. For some people, the Twelve Steps are their spiritual path and the self-help group is their Higher Power. There is often more ability to cope with a rough period in one's life when one has a set of guidelines to replace their old automatic patterns of behavior and/or when there is support available from other people who are understanding.

Some people dislike the concept of a Higher Power or spirituality. It takes a lot for some people to accept this idea, especially if they have rejected religion or if they think of it as having to do with *spirits*. But people often use this metaphor when they talk about someone having a lot of spirit or when they speak of the spirit of the law, etc. In this sense, it means that there is an essence or a fundamental nature of something, a sense of something. It really does not have to be so mystical or strange. It can be experienced as a kind of attunement or understanding.

There is great power in experiencing attunement and understanding. The word spiritual comes from the Latin, meaning *of the air* or *to breathe*. That is, it refers to things which, like a breath of air, are not tangible or concrete. It is there, everyone knows it, you can feel it, but it is difficult to explain. Spirituality, as used in the modern sense, also seems to me to carry the connotation of living a particular path. It is not necessarily a religious path, but it is a deeply felt experience. It is a kind of inspiration (the root of the word inspire is *to breathe in*) and one can achieve this just by watching a sunset. It is this kind of spirituality that is evident in the authors of this book. They are working hard to live their spirituality and to convey their inspiration to others. Their inspiration is the Twelve Steps as they understand them in relation to being survivors of sexual trauma.

I do not know of another book that specifically relates the Twelve Steps to survivors of sexual abuse which is more clear and readable than this one. Ms. Sweeting and Ms. Gust have done a great service to the many people who are struggling to resolve their traumas and to live out the rest of their lives safely and comfortably; in peace. They have covered many areas of this topic which needed to be explored and addressed by survivors themselves. This is clearly a needed and valuable book. I recommend it highly to all survivors, their families and friends, as well as to those professionals who work with them in their healing.

Charles R. Stern, Ph.D.
Clinical Psychologist and Clinical Neuropsychologist

Dr. Stern has been working with survivors of sexual abuse for over 20 years.

Introduction

The dictionary defines incest as *sexual intercourse between persons too closely related to marry legally.* This definition of incest implies consent, and this is not necessarily, and perhaps even rarely, the case. In this book we are going to broaden the definition of incest to include cases of sexual abuse where the perpetrator is in a position of authority over his/her victim. In this book, these two terms—incest and sexual abuse—will be used almost interchangeably. The incest and sexual abuse we are going to discuss here are the ugly kinds—the abuse no one ever wants to talk about: parents sexually abusing their children; teachers or ministers abusing children placed in their care; date rape or rape by a spouse; babysitters molesting their charges. And this is only the tip of the iceberg. For our purpose, sexual abuse and incest have very broad definitions.

Sexual abuse/incest is a violation of trust between an adult and an unsuspecting person, or any person in a position of authority who abuses someone else's trust and/or violates their body. It is any form of sexual abuse, whether overt or covert, which is directed at someone who is an unwilling participant, or is too young to make a rational choice. This abuse can be obscene talk or gestures, rape, fondling, sodomy, oral sex or intercourse. Sexual abuse happens between a man and a female victim; a man and a male victim; a woman and a female victim; and a woman and a male victim. Both sexes are perpetrators, and both sexes are victims.

Sexual abuse can happen to a person at any age. Some people are abused before birth. Others are abused as young adults or older. Our stories or histories are different, but the pain we feel is the same.

This book was written because we—Pat and Jean—were victims of abuse, and we want to share our experience, strength and hope for a better today with other abuse victims.

We have lived our lives hiding this dark secret of abuse, feeling guilt and shame that really did not belong to us. It is time to be honest and open about what happened, and how it has affected our lives. And, it is time to find out what we can do about it. The past is history and beyond our control. The future will take care of itself, if we take care of ourselves now, in the present. Right now is all we ever truly have.

These are our choices. We can continue to exist as victims, expecting and getting negative results in every situation and from everyone, and bemoaning our fate: "If only my life could have been different. If only someone could have loved me." We can get to the survivor stage, when we realize that, even though it was horrible, we lived through it; perhaps because of it we became stronger. Or we can live as recovered people: happy, joyous, and free, truly living and experiencing life.

Yes, bad things were done to us. Yes, our spirits and souls were robbed. Yes, we were victims—but we don't have to be victims anymore. What are we going to do about it? How can we change our attitude and outlook on life? These are the questions we—Pat and Jean— asked, and the answer for us was to work the Twelve Steps of Alcoholics Anonymous as they pertain to our lives as sexual abuse survivors.

This book was written for all victims of sexual abuse who would like to become recovered people. It is for women and for men. It is for people who were abused at all different ages: from 0 to 100. It isn't an issue of gender or age; this book has been written to help everyone who still suffers.

This book was also written for some very special people— the small, lost children within all of us. When we were abused, our spirits and inner selves went into hiding, hoping that somehow that would save them from the horror that was happening in their lives. Somehow we have to contact those small, frightened persons and convince them that it's okay to come out now, that the abuse is over, and it's time to live. We need to integrate all aspects of ourselves, and the best way we know how to do that is to use the Twelve Steps of Recovery.

Whether you have always remembered being abused or whether you have only begun to have memories, these Steps can help you. Some people found being abused so terrible that they blocked all memories of the abuse out of their minds. But these memories are still inside each of us, festering and causing problems in our lives that we cannot understand. Clinicians believe that if someone only has a feeling that they may have been sexually abused, the chances are very strong that they actually were. Others of us have always had a conscious knowledge that the abuse happened, but we did not realize the long-lasting effects it had on our lives.

It is time now to look at this core issue, to deal with it to the best of our ability. We have all suffered in silence too long. We can't change the past, but we can change our automatic emotional and behavioral responses to it. We were victims then, but the adult or the perpetrator was the responsible party—the guilt is theirs. We are the responsible people in our lives now. We are the only ones who can put our lives back together. We are the only ones who can reach those small, frightened children within us and give them back their lives.

We had no power when we were being abused. These Twelve Steps will give us power now, and the ability to change and to live.

As each of us proceeds through these Steps, we must remember that this is exactly what they are: steps that build on each other. Going through each one gives us the foundation, willingness and ability to move on to the next Step. When we are working Step Three, we should not be thinking about Step Eight. We do not yet have the ability, or perhaps the willingness, to do Step Eight. That's because we haven't gotten there yet. We don't learn algebra by reading and working on the first three chapters of an algebra book, then skipping to Chapter Eight. We would be lost and floundering. We must give ourselves time to take each Step separately, for each one prepares us to move on to the next Step.

We don't have to do any of these Steps perfectly. That isn't possible. These Steps are not something we're going to do one time and be finished with forever. It isn't like a twelve-week course at school; it is a Twelve Step change for the rest of our lives. Hopefully, each of us will find in them a manner of living that we can pursue and preserve for the rest of our lives. Only the first Step can be done perfectly: admitting powerlessness and unmanageability. For the remainder of our journey, we will move progressively toward each goal, one day at a time.

The questions at the end of each chapter are intended to be used in exploring each person's life as it has been affected by being abused. They are not a form of therapy, nor are they intended to replace therapy. They are intended to enhance each Step by offering suggestions we can keep in mind as we work our way through the Twelve Steps. It may be helpful for each reader to get a notebook and write the answers out fully, not merely using a *yes-no* format. The questions, and your individualized responses, may suggest new avenues you need to explore—or old ones you're still trying to avoid.

As you proceed through the questions, stop any time you begin to feel overwhelmed. Take a break; you can always return to the questions later. Talk with a friend, sponsor or therapist about what happened. Nothing in this book is intended to hurt or re-abuse you. Be gentle with yourself and go at a safe pace for you.

Working the Twelve Steps has helped us—Pat and Jean—to change our lives around completely. We are everlastingly grateful to the founders for starting it all, and we thank the people of A.A. for sharing their program with us, and for allowing us to share it with you.

The founders of A.A. discovered that they could help other alcoholics when doctors, ministers and other caring people couldn't, because they knew exactly what the alcoholic was feeling. We have found this to be true for us as sexual abuse survivors. It's true that to understand how a person feels, you have to "walk a mile in their shoes." We have been there. We believe you, and love you, and hope this book will help you on your personal journey to recovery.

Benefits of Using the Twelve Steps

▸ People, places and things won't change, but we can and will put manageability back in our lives.

▸ We can accept the past as the past, and have a strong identity of who we are today.

▸ Once we feel peaceful and serene, we can accept criticism or praise as a yardstick to measure our lives.

▸ Our experiences can help other survivors of abuse who must walk the same path. We will comfort each other, as we are not alone anymore.

▸ As we walk through the darkness and into the light, we can see our strengths and weaknesses as part of our humanness.

▸ We can focus on our individual recoveries without being envious of the achievements of others.

▸ Through the many changes in our lives, we will find that we have rights and choices.

▸ By validating our own existences, we will no longer depend on others to define who we are.

▸ By developing a normal, functional self-image, we can learn to believe in ourselves and need no longer fear authority figures.

▸ By lowering our self-imposed barriers, we can experience change, peace and serenity.

▸ We can acknowledge that we each have the right to face life and express our feelings without fear of the consequences or punishment.

▸ Through our Higher Power, who will not abandon us, we can learn to love and nurture ourselves.

Step One

We admitted we were powerless over sexual abuse—
that our lives had become unmanageable.

Step One

Admitting that we are powerless over sexual abuse is very difficult, and yet it is vital to our recovery. This is the beginning of the work we have to do in order to grow into the individuals which we are all capable of becoming.

When we were children, we thought that we had control, that somehow we were causing the abuse to happen, that we were *bad kids.* We felt that if we just were obedient enough, quiet enough, bright enough, whatever enough, that the abuse would stop and we would be safe. We had the feeling that nothing we did was ever good enough, or that if we had been better, the abuse would not have happened at all. We have to realize that none of this is true.

There was absolutely nothing we could have done to stop the abuse. We must believe with our whole heart, mind and spirit that there was nothing we could have done. We were helpless victims, no matter what our age at the time we were abused; the adult perpetrators had full control, and bear full responsibility. They were the ones who took our power and control, and in return gave us shame, guilt, and a secret to keep at all costs, even at the cost of making us feel like victims for the rest of our lives.

Sometimes we can't admit to powerlessness because we don't believe there is anything to admit at all. We use all sorts of defense mechanisms: denying, blocking out, or minimizing what happened. When we do this, and we say things like, "It wasn't so bad. That person had it worse." or, "I feel like something happened, but it couldn't have." we are trying to deny the reality of the anguish and the long-lasting effects of sexual abuse. We are trying to stay in control. When we use such childlike, magical thinking, we tell ourselves that as long as we stay in control, deny, or minimize, then we can believe it really didn't happen. We can pretend a little longer that our lives were okay and normal.

> **Eva said:** I knew I grew up in a dysfunctional family, but never even thought about or considered sexual abuse. But when the flashbacks started coming one right after the other, I found that every time I wanted not to believe it, I was denying my very existence. When I started considering that the memories might be true, the pounding headaches would stop for awhile.

Occasionally, some of us block our memories so effectively that they don't surface for years and years. Eventually though, memories do begin to return and we may actually have a difficult time believing or trusting in our own memories. Sometimes our families keep the denial system going.

> **Sally told us:** I remember my dad telling me I must be lying, that my grandfather would never do anything like that to me. My father still refuses to believe anything ever happened to me.

The people we should have been able to trust and turn to in times of need were often the very people who stole our trust and/or used our body for their own sick needs. Some of us never tried to tell anyone, because there was no one safe to tell. Some of us felt so guilty about the abuse that we were ashamed to tell anyone. Some of us were told by the perpetrator that the people we told would be harmed, or that we would be even more badly abused. Some of us hid the abuse so far down in the recesses of our minds that we had no conscious memories of the facts. All of this denying, blocking and minimizing has to end in order for us to get beyond the victim stage.

Although it is hard for many people to believe, some of us were also used by members of a cult or satanic worship group. In these cases, the abused were made to perform sexual acts with other cult members and/or animals. We were sometimes forced to drink blood or eat feces, or were covered with feces. Some ritual abuse survivors may also have been programmed to return to the cult at some later date. For those of us abused in this way, it is especially important to admit our absolute powerlessness over these events. We must hold the cult members completely responsible for their actions and beliefs.

Now is the time to be honest and to face the difficult truth, to finally admit that we were abused. This can be extremely painful, but it is necessary for us to walk through this pain, for on the other side a new freedom and a new happiness is waiting.

Many of us were little children at the time we were sexually abused. We never learned that we have control over our own destiny. We may still feel like we are only 6, 8 or 10 years old when we associate with our perpetrator, authority figures, or people who remind us of the perpetrator. As children, we felt helpless and hopeless. The initiators or perpetrators in our abuse were the ones who had control over our lives. As sexual abuse victims, we had no choice in how, when, where or even *if* we were to be abused. There were no choices at all for the victims.

> **Betty was raped by three policemen at a peace demonstration when she was 18:** I was fighting against the war in Vietnam and found out there was no peace and safety in my own country. I believed policemen were supposed to protect me. Now I am fighting a war inside my body and mind each and every day. I don't know what peace is anymore.

As abused children, we had no one to trust. When the adults in your life are abusing you, or aren't protecting you from the perpetrator, who is there to trust? It feels like nowhere is safe. We need to realize that children have no power over adults; they never did and they don't now.

The next time you see a 12-year-old child, or a 4-year-old, or an 8-year-old, look at them very closely. Look at their size and their strength. Compare it to yours as an adult. Try to remember how it felt to be that little and to have an adult abuse you. Only in fairy tales like *Jack in the Beanstalk* does someone little defeat the giant.

There was no way on earth we could have stopped the abuse from happening. All this time, we have been bearing the burden of toxic shame and guilt that doesn't belong to us. We were the victims. It is time now to admit and to accept that we had no power over those perpetrators.

Most of us stopped growing emotionally when the abuse started. Our bodies kept on getting larger, but our fragile inner selves were stunted. We may have developed sliding, split, adaptable or multiple personalities to contain and hold our hurting inner child. We may have felt like our stomachs had huge empty holes in them. We may have dissociated from pain, completely numbed our bodies, or created fantasy worlds.

> **Marianne recalls how she created her own bedtime stories:** Every night I would lie in bed imagining myself doing wonderful things like rescuing my family from a burning building—how everyone praised me and loved me. Or when things were bad, I'd pretend I had died and I planned my entire funeral. I pictured my parents and family crying and feeling awful. I was glad that they were finally feeling as bad as I did. Sometimes I would repeat the same story day after day, enjoying the warmth or the peace it gave me.

We may have felt like we were so broken and abused that no amount of glue, bandages or "all the king's horses and all the king's men" could put us together again. These inner children are still inside us somewhere, hoping that someday the world will be safe for them again. By admitting our powerlessness over the abuse, we can begin to set them free.

Even as adults, we are powerless over the abuse that happened to us. We still feel as helpless and hopeless as we did back then. We are powerless over the process that our subconscious mind is using to tell our conscious mind the facts regarding our sexual abuse. Sometimes we may dream so much at night that we wake up exhausted and find that our significant other has a fresh black eye, the bed is torn apart, and we don't know how any of it happened. Or we might be at work, and in the middle of a meeting suddenly have a sensation of being smothered and crushed. Whether by physical or sensory memories, or by complete flashbacks where we feel that we are back in the abuse situation, we are powerless to control the time or the place when these disturbing memories occur.

We are also powerless over the emotional abuse that we suffered. Our bodies were abused, but so were our minds, emotions, wills and spirits. So many of our automatic responses are the results of sexual abuse. When we hear harsh voices, we cringe. At night, when we see a large shadow surrounded by light in the doorway to our bedroom, we become paralyzed with fear. When we hear whispering or heavy footsteps, our hearts start to pound and our palms get sweaty. We expect criticism and negative reactions from other people. We expect verbal and emotional and maybe even physical abuse from others. We have very low self-esteem. We believe we are worthless.

In order to recover, we must realize we are powerless to change the person or persons in our lives who committed these horrid acts. They will never change simply because we want them to change. They have to find their own salvation and their own recovery.

Perhaps we were able to take control of our lives for a while, but at some point we started losing control. We'd get a little frayed around the edges, then one seam would burst, then another, until we were completely falling apart. In many cases, our financial situation was in disorder; our personal relationships were almost nonexistent; or we had to be hospitalized.

Our walls of denial were slowly disintegrating, brick by brick. Maybe we thought that when the actual abuse stopped, that this was the end of it. The physical aspect was over, therefore there was nothing to worry about anymore. Or maybe we thought that because it all happened so long ago we weren't being affected by it anymore. These are forms of denial and these beliefs have to change. We have to admit that our lives have been affected all though the years, and will continue to be affected until we do something about it. We need to stop our yesterdays from crashing into our todays and stealing our tomorrows.

Some of the ways that sexual abuse has affected our lives are more dramatic than others. Sometimes we look for parent figures to try to *get it right this time* and not be abused. Many of us enter into relationships with people who will abuse us, in effect re-creating our past over and over again. Some of us react by becoming sex addicts, jumping from partner to partner in a vain effort to get the affection we crave, or masturbating several times daily, trying to cope with our lives. Because being sexual was the only way we felt we could get the affection and love we needed from the adults in our lives, we have continued this pattern into our own adulthood. Others among us have become unable to enjoy sex at all, afraid and terrified by sexual relations with anyone, even our significant others. Some of us have become numb, able to perform sexually yet feeling nothing. We go through the motions of making love, all the while planning what to wear tomorrow, or thinking about the meeting we attended earlier. One day, finally, that's no longer enough for us. Our friends tell us about their wonderful sexual experiences and how terrific they felt, and we begin to long for fuller, richer lives for ourselves.

Many of us took on separate parts or personalities as a means of survival.

> **Fran shared:** My therapist helped me to realize the voices I had been hearing in my head all this time weren't normal thought processes, but multiple personalities. I had literally split into separate parts, separate people, in order to survive the ritual abuse I had suffered.

We have created fantasies to make up for the loss of our self-esteem and self-worth. We have created lies to cover up our hurts. We have created imaginary families and friends to help us survive.

Some of us nearly starved ourselves so we would look like asexual beings, trying to keep ourselves safe that way. Others among us have built walls of fat to protect ourselves from anyone admiring or wanting our bodies. We probably didn't consciously decide, "now I'll eat so much that I get really fat so no one will touch me," but eating can be very soothing. We may have used food or been given food to console ourselves after the abuse occurred, and stuffing down feelings with food soon became a habit.

> **Karen, abused by her mother for years, told us how she has used food:** I eased my pain in the bad times with food, I celebrated the good times with food. I eat now when I'm angry, tired, happy, or bored. Everything that happens in my life gives me a reason to eat.

Eventually we find ourselves eating all the time. Eating becomes an obsession, filling our every waking moment with thoughts of what we have already eaten, what we will be eating soon, how we'll cook it, how much of it we can have without anyone noticing. This gives us something else to think about instead of remembering or feeling the abuse we suffered.

Finally, after years of trying different diets and joining weight loss programs, losing weight only to regain it all back and sometimes more, we realize that this can't go on. It's time to face reality and accept that we can't stuff our pain and feelings down our throats any longer. We get *sick and tired of being sick and tired.* We hit bottom, our low point from where we can begin our climb back to sanity.

Creating chaos in our everyday lives is sometimes the way we have coped, because being crazy in a crazy world is what we're used to. If we can just keep busy enough, we don't have time to look inside or remember. Some people fill their every waking moment with *must-do* things. We can become workaholics, staying at our place of employment until 8:00 at night, then bringing home more work in our briefcases.

Even those of us who don't have a job outside our homes can be workaholics. We drive the kids to every activity available, become president of the P.T.A., run the local charity drive, become scout leaders, volunteer for the suicide hotline, never say no to any request for baked goods or craft items, then decide to join a local theatre group because we "have a little extra time." We go to bed at 1:00 a.m. exhausted, then get up and do it all over again. We talk about how busy we are and how tired we always are, yet keep on doing the same things again and again.

All such people have unmanageable lives. The only way to change such crazy behavior is to totally surrender, to admit to our inability to take care of ourselves in a healthy manner.

Ask yourself these questions:

Do I continually believe that the only thing the opposite sex wants is to abuse me?

Do certain days or dates on the calendar send me into a tailspin and I can't or don't remember why or how?

Do I feel aches and pains in many parts of my body for which medical science cannot find a cause?

Have I ever had anyone come up behind me wanting only to give me some affection, and I turned around jumping and shouting in their face?

This list can go on and on. Each of us can probably add many incidents and times when our lives were out of control.

Our lives are unmanageable. We tend to eat, sleep and live our lives in the victim role. All of these coping methods work for a while. But eventually we find that what once worked is no longer working. We choose not to be victims any longer. We believe that there must be a better life for us, and we need help to find it.

Step One is the first step in our process of change. It states the problem that has been standing in the way of our living a full, happy life. It is the base on which we will rebuild our lives. It says, "This is where I'm starting. This is what I used to be like."

There is no action required of us in this first step. We need only to admit. We need to acknowledge that we are and were powerless over sexual abuse. We need to believe that it wasn't our fault. It is time to look for new ways of coping and living. If even one aspect of our lives is unmanageable because of sexual abuse and we admit that, then we have done Step One. When we admit our powerlessness—that we have no control over sexual abuse—then we can move on to the next step in the process of recovery.

Step One Questions

▸ Do you believe that you caused your abuse, or that if you had just done something differently the abuse wouldn't have taken place?

▸ Did people tell you, as they abused you, that it was your own fault?

▸ When you see someone who reminds you of the perpetrator, do you get scared?

▸ Do you relive situations over and over again, trying to figure out a way to make it different?

▸ When you try to remember your childhood, do you draw a blank?

▸ Have you tried to deny to yourself that any abuse ever happened to you?

▸ Do you have flashbacks or body memories?

▸ Do you feel numb, unable to experience any emotion?

▸ Do you abuse alcohol or other drugs in an attempt to numb your feelings?

▸ Can you admit you were powerless over the situation as it was happening?

▸ Can you admit that you are powerless over the negative affects of being abused?

▸ Do you apologize to everyone for everything, no matter what the circumstances?

▸ Do you let others tell you what, how and when to do things?

▸ In your relationships with other people, do you have to be in control of every situation?

▸ Do you control your children with rigid rules and restrictions?

▸ Do you let your children *do their own thing* because you were stifled as a child?

▸ Do you take your anger out on family members by abusing your children or your spouse, physically, emotionally, or sexually?

▸ Do you abuse yourself physically, emotionally or sexually?

▸ Do you always seem to end up in relationships with people who will take advantage of you or abuse you somehow?

▸ Do you feel a constant sense of shame?

▶ Do you spend money that you don't have or have no means of obtaining?

▶ Do you gamble obsessively?

▶ Do you hoard your money, never spending anything, even for necessities?

▶ Do you get along with other people—spouse, children, boss, fellow-employees?

▶ Do you maintain rigid control over your life, never doing anything spontaneously?

▶ Do you believe that you are bad, or that you should be punished, because your body enjoyed the sexual attentions it received?

▶ Are you afraid of members of the opposite sex?

▶ Do you feel that if you don't have a lover you aren't worth anything?

▶ Do you cling to your lover, overwhelming him/her with attention and demands?

▶ Do you withhold sex from your lover because that feels like the only thing you have control over?

▶ Do you eat compulsively when you feel sad, happy, bored, tired—and then purge?

▶ Do you starve yourself in a mistaken belief that you are too fat?

▶ Do you allow yourself to take time off from work if you are sick?

▶ Do you feel like you are the only one who can get a job done right, whether at home, work, or in the community?

▶ Do you hold people at arm's length, never allowing anyone too close to the real you?

NOTES

Step Two

*We came to believe that a Power greater than ourselves
could restore us to sanity.*

Step Two

Step Two calls on us, as sexual abuse and incest survivors, to take a different direction in our lives. In Step One, we admitted to a human powerlessness that seems to leave us with no place to find the help we so badly need. This second Step tells us there is a power greater than ourselves that can restore us to sanity. It tells us that, if we believe, this power will give us back soundness of judgment and the ability to live our lives sanely, not like we have been: barely holding on, pretending to be normal and not doing too well at it.

What we need to work this Step is a willingness to believe, to take as true the affirmation stated in Step Two. If willingness is all we can manage right now, that's okay. If we can begin to trust, even a little, then we are "coming to believe." For some people, coming to believe is a slow process, evolving over a period of time. For others, believing in this power is a dramatic and sudden event. Each of us needs to take whatever time is necessary for a belief pattern to develop. However it happens for you, know that your recognition of and belief in a Higher Power will be the key to recovery, serenity and peace.

These Twelve Steps are not something we do one time and are finished with. They are a continual process through which we will grow, change and recover. This second Step is the structural and spiritual foundation upon which all the others are based. Without trusting that a Higher Power will be able to help, sustain and guide us, it might be difficult to make the Twelve Steps an integral part of our lives.

> **Mary, who had been raped at the age of 19, said:** When I first tried working these Steps, I'd do the two-step waltz. First I'd admit I was powerless, then I'd go out spreading the message and trying to help others. Step One to Step Twelve, then back again. Finally, after realizing that I was just as miserable as I'd ever been, I looked at Step Two. When I finally accepted that there was a power greater than myself, I was able to work through the rest of the Steps.

Our inability to trust or to believe may make it difficult to conceive that any thing or any being can help us. It may be hard because for so many years we have had to rely only on our strength of will. As children, we may have prayed many prayers to the adults' god, only to have those pleas go unanswered. Even while the abuse was taking place, we may have begged, "please someone, make it stop," but nothing changed. This makes it hard to believe that there's someone or something out there or deep within our essence listening to us.

Now it is time to take tiny steps in trust, outside ourselves and/or deeper into ourselves. We must come to know that, all our lives, through the good times and the bad times, a universal force has been keeping us alive so that one day we could become the healthy people we were meant to be. We must feel this at our inner-most core. We must believe it, so that our inner child finally can feel safe. It is time to stop abandoning ourselves, as we believe others have abandoned us. For each of us, a Higher Power is waiting to be found.

Until now, power and strength have been missing in our lives, power to be whole and complete people, strength to be responsible adults. Now we can begin to learn how to develop these attributes, but first we need to decide where the power is going to come from. Each of us needs to personally define *higher power*. This entity or force, whatever we choose to call it, will guide us on a path that will ultimately, in our personalized time frame, restore us to a healthy, happy life. And when we do choose a personal Higher Power, we allow that Power into every aspect of our lives.

We must recognize that operating on our ego alone has not given us the strength we need and the happiness we deserve. There must exist a power greater than ourselves, a spiritual reality that can support us in every step of our recovery. To change our negative habits and thought patterns, we need to turn to a power greater than we are. Many of us have tried to change at different periods in our lives, only to fall back into our old ways after a short time. With a Higher Power in our lives, taking an active role, and giving us strength, love and nurturing every day, we can change. We can improve our lives. We can be restored to sanity.

Some of us have confused the words trust, faith and control. The dictionary defines trust as a firm reliance; committed into the care of another; charge. Faith is defined as confidence, loyalty and allegiance to a system of beliefs. Control means a power to regulate, direct or dominate.

We were told by the sick people in our lives to put our trust in them. They would take care of us. They wanted us to believe that they knew what was best for us. They said they knew what we needed, even before we did. They told us to have faith only in them; that they had control of our lives. They tried to direct our thinking to fulfill their sick and perverted needs.

> **Joan, who was abused by her parish priest over the course of several years, said:** My abuser told me that he was God, and I believed him. There was no one answering

my prayers, so I figured he must be right. He told me that I was hopeless, not worth anything, and I believed that, too.

Those of us who were used in cult or ritual abuse were programmed to believe that the group was in control of our very souls and beings.

These were our gods out of fear, given to us when we were vulnerable. We are not children, adolescents or vulnerable adults any longer. Now is the time to decide just what our beliefs are, to choose a Higher Power consciously, as an adult. It makes little difference whether our Higher Power is found in a conventional religious setting or is some kind of force. Now is not the time to debate the existence of a Higher Power; our very lives depend on a simple belief in the goodness of a Higher Power.

We are now ready to take back control of our own destiny. We need to insert the pronoun, "I," back into our lives. We can trust our feelings for the first time, trusting in our *inner voice*. The power in which we choose to believe must be a power or force that we can trust and one with which we can have a personal, open and loving relationship. We no longer have to believe in someone else's definition of god. The faith practices of our parents need not influence us in our choice of a Higher Power.

> **Higher Power means different things to different people. To Sara, it meant a self-help group:** For a long time, I had to regard the Twelve-Step group I belonged to as my Higher Power. I had given up any belief in a supreme being, but I realized these people collectively were bigger, more knowledgeable, and stronger than I could ever be alone.

To others, it is the Higher Power of a traditional, formal religion: Catholic, Protestant, Jewish, Hindu. For someone else, it is love, or the power of the universe. How we define this power is our personal choice. Perhaps we associate the old concept of a Higher Power with the perpetrator or our old family system that didn't work. Perhaps we rebelled against that god.

> **Lisa cried:** Where was God when my father was molesting me week after week? Why did God let this happen?

Or perhaps we decided to distance ourselves from any association with the perpetrator or our family, deciding that "if they believe in that god, then I sure don't want to." Very young children see their parents as god-like, and if their parents abused them, why would they want to believe in a Higher Power at all? Now, as adults who are ready to change and to grow, we must risk believing that there is a power greater than ourselves that can and will help us, if we only ask.

If you don't have a ready concept of spiritual reality, there are many ways to find your own Higher Power. Some people write a letter or a want ad, listing all of the characteristics they want in a Higher Power. Then they visualize some entity entering their lives which matches their description. Some people put their Higher Power into human form; others believe there is a force in the universe that is their Higher Power. You could draw a picture of your Higher Power, and visualize that image when you talk with your Higher Power. Others have difficulty calling anything "god," so they think of their Higher Power as Good Orderly Direction.

> **Heidi shared:** I never had a best friend, so I imagined what it would be like to have someone I could tell everything to. I pretend that I have a special person who is always there for me, and I call this best friend God.

Talk with other people who have discovered a personal Higher Power, and ask them what they did and how it worked for them. The idea is to make our Higher Power personal, someone or something that we can call on at any time. That's the kind of Higher Power we need to help us get through this life and really live, not just exist.

This journey through the Twelve Steps is not part of a conventional religious theology. It is a spiritual pathway to serenity and peace. What we are asked to do in this Step is to define a Higher Power that will work for and with us on our journey into recovery. When we talk about this spiritual journey, we aren't referring to religion. We are talking about a spiritual awakening, a mental change that takes place through working these Twelve Steps. This spiritual awakening means things pertaining to our attitudes and actions, not what Higher Power we believe in. These Steps will change us. When we have completed these Twelve Steps, our attitudes and outlook on life will change. We will have a change in our thinking and the way we feel. And because our attitudes and thinking change, our behavior will change, too. That means we will begin to live sanely and rationally. This is a promise of better things to come.

To be restored to sanity, we must first acknowledge the insanity of our pre-recovery life.

> **Tom stated:** I would really like to get married, but every time I begin to get close to a woman, I see my mother's face on that woman and I run away and hide. Does every woman look like my mother? I feel like I am going crazy.

There are many definitions of insanity. One definition that seems to fit many of us is: continuing to do the same thing over and over again, and expecting different results. Another example of insanity is: fantasizing about changes in our past, in our families, and in the perpetrator, when in reality we can't change them at all. Repeatedly entering into relationships where the significant other is similar to the perpetrator, hoping to rewrite our history, is another good sign that reliance on a Higher Power is needed.

It is also important to recognize and to accept that we *were* once sane. To be restored means to be put back again to something we once were. Maybe we wonder if we ever had sanity in our lives, and doubt that we did. For some of us that is close to the truth. But even if we have to go back in our lives to the moment of conception, at least then there was some sanity for us. With the help of a Higher Power, we can be restored to that spiritual, peaceful calm which we need in our lives today.

Some of us might still believe that we aren't worth restoring to sanity, that we don't deserve it.

> **Hope recalled:** My mother told me I would not amount to anything. I was not worthy even to consume air. She told me if I talked to anyone about the physical and emotional abuse she gave me, I would be locked up like Aunt Mary. I can't even begin to imagine how she could have named me Hope.

Such thinking must change, because each of us, no matter what our past, deserves to be sane and rational. We are good people who have been seriously hurt, and we deserve to have wonderful things happen to us.

We can be restored to sanity. Our Higher Power can lead us to change the way we feel about ourselves and to change our attitudes toward other people. Our Higher Power can transform us from a victim into a survivor. Our Higher Power can change us from a wounded being to a healthy person, and re-program our thinking so we can become a complete person: healthy in mind, body, soul and spirit.

Sanity for us is soundness of judgment; sanity is making decisions that make sense in today's reality, not in yesterday's memories. Sanity is living daily without feeling crazy, without feeling dirty, without the negative thoughts that run through our minds constantly. Sanity is knowing peace and serenity in our lives today.

Insanity is like being in hell, and being restored to sanity means climbing out of that hell, one step at a time. The joys of sanity are unimaginable to us while we're living in our pain. When we're surrounded by and filled with insanity, we can't imagine anything being different. But with our Higher Power's help, we can be restored to sanity.

This Step asks us to consider all the alternatives available to us for believing in a Higher Power. It asks us to consider choosing someone or something to guide us, to direct us, and to restore us to sanity. We must keep an open mind and be realistic in our thinking. We have already taken one risk by admitting our powerlessness over sexual abuse. Now we must take another risk and search out our Higher Power. We keep seeking and searching. We make our decision based on our personal faith and trust. We have full control over all of our choices, and our rights are being restored to our control. In Step One we acknowledged the problem. In Step Two we find the solution: we learn, or re-learn, to have faith that something or someone more powerful than we are will help us whenever we need it.

Step Two Questions

▶ Do you have a Higher Power, a universal force, or a force beyond yourself in your life right now?

▶ At some time in your life, did you reject the idea of a personal Higher Power?

▶ Did you ask a Higher Power for help while you were being abused?

▶ Did you feel that your Higher Power was ignoring you?

▶ What kind of spiritual beliefs did you receive from your caretakers while you were growing up?

▶ Do those beliefs work for you now?

▶ Do you believe that you can't give your power away or you will be abused again?

▶ If you had a Higher Power, what would it be like?

▶ Do you believe in a Higher Power, but don't believe that Higher Power is interested in your life?

► Were you told that your abuser was God?

► Were you told that God would never help you?

► Are you afraid to believe in anything outside of yourself?

► Do you believe that there might be something somewhere that has more power than you do?

► Is there a force or spirit deep within your being that might give you strength when you need it?

► Are you willing to rely on that source of strength?

► Are you willing to take the time necessary to seek out and find your Higher Power?

► Are you willing to be open to whatever comes as an answer to your seeking?

► Are you willing to believe that your personal Higher Power cares for you?

► What would it take for you to believe in a force greater than yourself?

► If you can believe in a Higher Power, do you believe that your Higher Power will restore you to sanity?

► Are you willing to let your Higher Power guide your life?

► Do you still believe that you have handled things just fine on your own?

► Are you afraid to trust anyone or anything but yourself?

► Are you a member of a church or religious organization?

► Are your spiritual needs being met through that organization?

► Do you feel that something fundamental is lacking in your life?

► Are you willing to consider believing in a Higher Power?

► Can you conceive that a force beyond yourself is ready to help you?

NOTES

Step Three

*We made a decision to turn our will and our lives over
to the care of our Higher Power,
as we understood that Power.*

Step Three

Step Three is the transition step between the cognitive steps—Step One when we admit; Step Two when we come to believe—and the action steps that remain. We are thinking beings, whether or not we are aware of all our thoughts, and all action is preceded by thought. This is the Step in which we will begin the change from reacting, feeling, then thinking individuals into people who think, feel, and then react.

We've admitted we have a problem: the horrible results of sexual abuse or incest that have permeated every aspect of our lives. We're coming to believe that a power greater than ourselves will restore us to sanity. Now we are deciding to trust that power with our will and our lives, our thinking and our actions. This is the beginning of a faith walk with *our personal Higher Power.*

We consciously choose to change our thinking. We each make this decision on a daily basis and reinforce this decision until it becomes a part of our daily routine. Some of us can only begin the process by hoping that there is a power greater than ourselves. We keep hoping until we want to believe in that power. Then we start believing; and finally we know that there is a power greater than we are. How we do that is not the issue; what matters is that we get out of our own way and seek our own personal spiritual force.

We have to turn our entire lives over to the care of a force beyond ourselves. We can't just turn over some parts and retain others. It must be a complete and total surrender of our will and our lives.

> **Charlotte had become addicted to alcohol and compulsive eating as a result of being abused as a child:** I joined Alcoholics Anonymous and turned my drinking over to God. Then I joined Overeaters Anonymous and turned my eating over to God. For a while, I was doing okay, but I never really seemed to get the peace and serenity that I saw in others. I was just 'not drinking or eating.' Finally, I came to realize that I had to give up control over the sexual abuse, too. I didn't want to; that seemed too scary. I was willing to trust God with everything but that. With my sponsor's help, I began to release control over this last aspect of my life, and my life became calmer. I guess I really did need to give up totally.

This Step requires us to trust our Higher Power entirely. This means that we will depend on our Higher Power, not like we were dependent on our parents or other authority figures, but in a healthy dependence, with us knowing that whatever happens, we will be safe and protected. Trusting our Higher Power doesn't mean that we just sit back and relax, waiting to be magically taken care of. We still have to put forth effort; we still have to do the footwork; but then we leave the outcome to this force beyond ourselves.

Making decisions, especially a major one like this, can be very difficult for sexual abuse survivors. Because we weren't given any choices earlier in our lives, we never learned how to make healthy decisions. Or we made decisions, then agonized over them for days and days, wondering if we had made the *right* decision. As a result of working these Steps, we will be able to make decisions, because we will always be safe now that we have faith in a power greater than we are. We are going to change from being people who never trusted anyone into people who trust, even if just a little bit, in a Higher Power as we perceive it to be.

This can be very frightening and totally different from our normal way of thinking. All our lives, we felt we had to stay in control or we would surely die. We felt that if we ever let down our guard, even a tiny bit, someone would use and abuse us again.

> **Mary's father molested her every weekend for years. She said:** I was sure that if I let myself relax for even a moment, something awful would happen to me. Ever since I was abused, I've operated on the principle of "I can do it, and I don't need anyone or anything to help me." I'm so grateful that I don't have to live that way anymore.

Perhaps it seemed like every time we trusted someone, they hurt us. They tried to destroy us. But the Higher Power of our understanding will not hurt us. We were taught during the abuse to trust the wrong people. We now consciously decide to change this pattern of behavior. Now it's time to believe that we can trust, that we can turn over our control, and still be safe. Any time we need the strength to get through difficult situations, we can call on our Higher Power, and know that it will enable us to do whatever it is we have to do.

This Step may cause us to begin the grieving process and to feel a longing for the things we have missed in our lives: friends, the ability to trust, feeling any emotions, feeling safe. We may grieve the loss of our family of origin, or the loss of our control to others.

> **Betty was confused about what it meant to be a complete individual, to be in control of her own destiny:** I thought everyone dealt with life by letting the stronger people make all the decisions. I thought I was supposed to be weak and dependent. No one ever told me it was okay for me to be in charge of my life.

Those of us who have experienced dissociative disorders may mourn the loss of time and reality. We may have to grieve the loss of our childhood and our faith in other people.

We learn to have patience with ourselves, and to give ourselves the time necessary to come to know ourselves. We need time to get in touch with the feelings and memories we have blocked for many long years. These Steps do not come with a specific time frame in which they must be completed. We allow all the time necessary for our Higher Power to nurture and heal the deep wounds that sexual abuse left us with. We allow our Higher Power—as we understand it—to do for us what we have not been able to do for ourselves.

We must not think of this Step as one of surrender. We are not being asked to give up. We are being asked to trust a force beyond ourselves to guide our thinking and our actions. We can always go back to our old ways and take our will and lives back into our control if we wish. We have done this many times before, to our detriment.

Our Higher Power does not want to manipulate our lives, but to help us to become the people we were always meant to be. We are like the rowers in a small boat. We row and row and row some more, hoping we're heading in the right direction, but usually only going in circles. Suddenly we have a helping force at the tiller, guiding us into a safe harbor that we hadn't even known existed.

Our own defiant willfulness and stubbornness has gotten us this far in our lives.

> **John had been abused by his babysitter until his family moved when he was seven:** I decided as I got older that no one would ever take advantage of me or my body again. I decided that even if it meant never letting anyone close to me again, that was what I would do to keep myself safe.

Now we need to let go of our need to be in charge, and let our Higher Power be the boss in our lives.

Linda shared: There is such a relief in knowing that I don't have to be in charge anymore, that I don't have to manipulate and twist and turn, trying to control results and people and things so that I will be safe and so that I will get what I want. Now I realize that I may not know the whole picture, that everything that happens has a purpose. I've come to accept that eventually everything turns out to be what I need, not necessarily what I want.

Step Three sounds simple, but it is not always easy to do. For some of us, it will take a daily re-commitment. Others may have to re-commit on an hourly basis; or maybe minute by minute, sixty times an hour, twenty-four hours every day. We may need to remind ourselves over and over, "I'm trusting in my Higher Power on this," until we make it such a habit that trusting comes automatically.

Sandra struggled for some time with this concept of trusting a god of her understanding: It was very hard for me to see or believe that God was working daily in my life. Finally, someone at a Twelve Step meeting suggested I use a *god box*, and write down all my daily problems and put them in this box. I thought they were kidding, but I tried doing it. At the end of one month, I pulled out all my bits and pieces of paper. I was amazed at the number of problems that were solved, seemingly without my intervention at all. I had to put some papers back in the god box, but my faith in God was intensified because there were fewer papers to put back than to throw away.

Perhaps we will begin trusting a force beyond ourselves with little decisions, gradually working up to trusting our Higher Power with major events in our lives. But hold on for the time needed to complete this very important Step. We don't want to quit just as our miracle is about to happen, and happen it will. This Higher Power—as you understand it—is willing to accept you as you are and give you all the time, nurturing, love and attention you need.

We gain some wonderful benefits from working this Step. We will be free from worry for the first time. We can stop fretting about what happened in the past, because we finally accept that it's over and we can't change it. We don't have to be concerned about what will happen to us in the future, because we know that we are always safe with our Higher Power working in us and through us. This gives us a wonderful sense of security, knowing that we will be able to handle anything that comes our way because we have an invisible strength behind us. We don't have control over any results, so we can give up trying to make everything turn out the way we want it to. We still make plans and goals, but we leave the results up to that force beyond ourselves. Our Higher Power will help us to do things that we never dreamed possible on our own.

We will gradually lose our fear, especially our fear of trusting others. As we give up control to our Higher Power, we see that it does work, that we are safe and protected for the first time in our lives.

> **Jackie told us about her dreams that were shattered after her friend's father raped her:** I had always planned to go to college after graduation. After he raped me, though, I felt so stupid for letting that happen that I gave up my dreams and went to work as a secretary. Now, twenty years later, because of these Twelve Steps and trusting in my Higher Power, I am making my dreams come true. I graduate next month from college, and have been accepted into graduate school. I never would have been brave enough to go back to school without the help of my Higher Power.

As soon as we are comfortable with this Step and have acted on this decision, we see ourselves and our view of the world changing in peace and love for the first time. As we silently and slowly release our lives to the care of our Higher Power, we may begin to feel our hurting inner child come into our conscious minds. For the very first time we may know the fears and confusion our inner child has always known: the internal war of sexual abuse still rages within us. This war goes on silently, the way we think and feel today. Our inner child learned the harsh reality of this world too soon and may not remember when there was a time to laugh and play. We aren't going to be able to stuff this child away again as we did when we were being abused. Today is the beginning of a new life with ourselves, our Higher Power and our inner child.

As we begin to experience nurturing, peace and love for the first time, it is important for our inner child to get to know them, too. We need to re-parent ourselves, using the same patience and understanding that our Higher Power is using to nurture and love us. In this manner, we give to ourselves what the adults in our lives did not. Just as parents should guide their young ones to become free individuals, our Higher Power will guide us in becoming the whole individuals we were meant to be, integrated for the first time with love and a sense of security.

This Step will help us to get in touch with our true feelings and with how we perceive ourselves in relation to the people in our lives. It will help us to realize how we react to other people, places and things, and how we fit into the universe as living, feeling human beings.

Step Three is one of willingness and hope. This is when we become willing to do something about the effects of the past and about how we are living now. This is when we begin changing from our victim roles into recovered people. This Step gives us hope that we can change, that it will be safe to change and that we will become stronger, healthier, healed people as a result of that change.

Step Three Questions

▶ Is it difficult for you to make decisions?

▶ Do you spend days agonizing over minor decisions?

▸ After you make a decision, do you obsessively worry about whether it was the right one?

▸ Can you let your Higher Power into every aspect of your life?

▸ Are you willing to give your Higher Power some parts of your life, but not all?

▸ Are you willing to turn your thinking over to your Higher Power?

▸Do you believe that you must still control certain aspects of your life?

▸ Can you share your pain and sorrow with that force beyond yourself?

▸ Are you willing to take action to change your life?

▸ Do you think that changes will come about with no effort on your part?

▸ Do you believe that things will magically change?

▸ Do you trust that your Higher Power will take care of you?

▸ Are you afraid to trust anyone to take care of you?

▸ Are you willing to trust your Higher Power with the results of your actions?

▸ Are you willing to think before you act or react?

▸ Are you willing to feel before you act or react?

▸ Are you willing to change your thinking?

▸ Does being dependent on someone or something other than yourself scare you?

▸ Are you afraid to trust your Higher Power with your life?

▸ Are you willing to give yourself all the time you need to heal?

▸ Do you feel that you have to be cured by tomorrow at the latest?

▸ Do you trust yourself?

▸ Do you trust other people?

▸ Do you trust certain people just because they are authority figures?

▸ Can you see where your control ends and trust begins?

▸ Can you distinguish between deciding to trust your Higher Power and having other people take charge of your life, whether you like it or not?

▸ Are you still giving your will over to people who don't deserve to even be in your life?

▸ Do you know that, at any time you want, you can take back your pain and hurt?

NOTES

Step Four

*We made a searching and fearless moral
inventory of ourselves.*

Step Four

Step Four is the first action step on our journey through the Twelve Steps. We will write a searching and fearless inventory of ourselves; to search means *to look into or over carefully and thoroughly in an effort to find or discover something.* There is no negative connotation to that definition. We are asked only to seek out ourselves, not to cut ourselves into little pieces. We are going to look at patterns of actions, reactions, and behaviors that have developed over the years and are now a part of us. We will not be searching alone, for Step Two and Step Three have introduced us to our personal Higher Power, who can help us get to know ourselves better. With the help of our Higher Power, we will explore the positive and negative aspects of ourselves, and how they influence our lives.

The fearless part of this inventory may be the hardest part for us; we have known fear for such a long time that it has become an integral part of our makeup. Some of our fears may include feeling that if someone were to know us for who we really are, they would run away forever. We have been afraid to look at the distorted picture of ourselves that the perpetrators of our abuse forced us to see; we are afraid of what long-put-aside horror we might relive if we force ourselves to write a thorough inventory. But, just as our Higher Power knows all our secrets, so there is a part of each of us that still remembers the terrible things we have tried so hard to forget.

Our very survival has, at times, depended on building and then maintaining the great walls of denial we have built for ourselves, but, try as we might, the simple fact is that we don't like ourselves; we would rather be anyone else but a person who has lived through the horrors of sexual abuse. And yet, we *have* lived through that horror, and now we will learn to like ourselves.

The *moral* part of this Step refers to our new ability to distinguish between what is good and what is bad for us; what is fair and equitable; what is right for us now, at this time and in this place in our lives. We aren't judging ourselves on what our past performance has been. We are examining our past so we can change what we are today, not our history. Many of the patterns in our lives today exist because of our past, but we can't go back and change that past. We can only change our attitudes and reactions toward it. By finally putting the blame for our abuse squarely on the perpetrator, we will free ourselves for the more important task of accepting responsibility for the way we live our lives today.

By writing this inventory, we hope to gain better insight into just what shortcomings we need to change and how our shortcomings have caused us to harm others. We need to actually put our inventories down in writing, because through the years we have learned to suppress many things: feelings, attitudes, even actual events. If we try to keep the reality separate from what we have tried to make ourselves believe for so long, we will likely continue to fool ourselves into minimizing what happened to us. By forcing ourselves to write out the facts, we can begin to deal with them.

Sue had been raped by her boyfriend one night after she told him she was breaking up with him. She shared: Last week at my meeting, I was sitting at a Fourth-Step table and mentioned that I had never taken an inventory, but I do a mini-inventory in my head each night. One of the other members asked me why I hadn't done a Fourth-Step Inventory. She said I was jumping from Step Three to Step Ten and missing a whole lot of healing in between. I went home that night and started on my Step Four, telling myself that I would never sit at an inventory table again and have to admit that I had never done a Step Four. Now I'm really thankful my friend talked with me. I really found out what a difference an inventory can make. I now have an excellent point of reference to continue with the rest of the Steps.

When we write down our inventory, there is nowhere to hide the truth; it will come out, regardless of our intentions.

Alice told us: It's an amazing thing what happens when I pick up a pen and some paper and start writing. I start out with one sentence like "I'm angry at my sister," and end up with "so that's why I've always reacted that way in that situation." Sometimes my writing will take an entirely different tangent from where I thought I was heading. The true difficulty always surfaces. It's absolutely incredible.

In Step Three we agreed we would trust our Higher Power with our will and our lives. This Step demonstrates our trust in our Higher Power. We know that we will always be safe with our Higher Power, so it will be safe to write this inventory. No one will hurt us; no one will abuse us. Now is the time to write down our secrets, the things we never told anyone before. This is our opportunity to reveal everything: things that were done to us, and things that we did to others.

We keep in mind as we write that we are writing only for ourselves and for our Higher Power. No one will edit this, no one will ever read this.

Tony, whose older sister abused him as a child, told his sponsor why he didn't want to write an inventory: I didn't want to write anything down anywhere because my mother would always correct my letters for spelling and punctuation and mail them back to me.

His sponsor helped him to realize that this program was for him personally and no one else: No one else will ever see my inventory. And my Higher Power doesn't grade my life on spelling and punctuation. My Higher Power accepts me as being the best person I can be, right now, flaws and all.

When we get to Step Five, we will share this inventory; for right now, it's private. We're doing these Steps one at a time, not anticipating or worrying about what's next.

This inventory is just what the word implies: a listing of what we have in stock; what we've learned; the actions, behaviors, and beliefs that we were taught and that are now counterproductive. The techniques we once used to survive only serve now to hinder our growth. The purpose of these Twelve Steps is to help us change our lives, but we can't change anything until we know what needs changing; awareness is the first step in change. This Fourth-Step Inventory will be the beginning of that awareness.

Some of us see this Step as a stop sign in our journey. We move along fine, then come up against this Step, panic, and put the brakes on. We let the thought of writing this inventory, or perhaps the thought of sharing this inventory with another, scare us so much that our recovery is stalled. We make excuses like, "I didn't do Step One thoroughly enough," or Step Two, perhaps, anything to put off writing an inventory.

If this kind of delay feels right to us, that is okay. How long it takes to write an inventory differs from person to person. Some of us will sit down and write our inventory in three or four hours. Or it might take a couple of weeks or months. However long it takes, the important thing is that we *do it.* We won't get anywhere in our recovery until we write an inventory, and this is the best reason to do it.

> **Mary said:** Something I've heard at meetings is that the only reason you do Step Four is so that you can get on to Step Five. And the only reason to do Step Five is to get to Step Six, and so on. The point is that we do these Steps, all of them, not just the first couple that seem easy.

One of the most important aspects of this Step is that we *begin*. A reason often given for stalling on Step Four is that people are afraid of what will be uncovered by their inventory. However, we aren't given anything that we can't handle right now—our minds are kind. We already know—or at least strongly suspect—that we are victims of incest or sexual abuse. By falling back on our Higher Power's strength, we will be able to cope with whatever else may come up. Those of us who have someone supportive in our lives, besides our Higher Power, might ask that person to sit with us while we write our inventory, just for moral support.

Another reason given for not writing an inventory is procrastination and/or perfectionism. A lot of us regularly put things off, especially anything that might be painful. This means of avoiding pain is one of our character defects. Through this Step, we learn to trust our Higher Power to give us the courage to get through anything, painful or not.

> **Valerie had been abused by four out of the seven males in her family. She told us:** After the pain I went through as a child, I will do anything to avoid pain now. "No pain, no gain," might be true for others, but for me, forget it. If it's likely to be painful, I want no part of it.

Perfectionism has two aspects: fear of failure and fear of success. With fear of failure, we're afraid that we won't get it right, and we'll screw up again—usually because someone has told us that we will always goof up everything we ever try.

With fear of success, we're afraid that if we are proven capable of taking care of ourselves, then we will have to do that all of the time. It is hard to feel that we must always succeed. It's important to acknowledge these feelings, ask our Higher Power for strength and courage, then go ahead and write our inventory anyway.

We should also remember that we are not writing another *Gone with the Wind.* This is an inventory—a listing—not a novel. We should write it thoroughly, but we should also be willing to call a halt somewhere. Once we've covered our life up until the present, then it is done. What we forget in this inventory, we can always cover in another inventory, be it our Step Ten daily inventory, or a mini-Step Four.

Most of what we write will not be a surprise, but it will help us see why we do so many of the things we do. Many of us blame others for our actions: "she made me do that," or "he made me angry." This inventory helps us see that quite often people were reacting to us and our actions, rather than simply treating us badly out of spite. *(This does not pertain to the abusers in our lives. They were abusing us for their own reasons, not because of anything we did. Remember, the responsibility for our abuse rests with the perpetrator. However, the resulting emotions, and the resulting behavior patterns we have developed belong to us, and these are the things we seek to change.)*

This inventory probably won't reveal anything that hasn't been done before by or to someone else. One of the wonderful aspects of a Twelve-Step group is that we find we are not unique, that others have experienced similar things and have similar feelings. Those of us who do not belong to a Twelve-Step group might find it harder to believe, but we are not alone. Millions of people have been abused. Each story is different, but the emotions and attitudes the abuse leaves behind are the same.

Notice that this Step says *inventory of ourselves.* This means that we are looking at our behaviors and attitudes, not at those of others. Certainly other people's actions will be mentioned, because they have had an all-pervasive effect on our lives. However, we look at our inventory, what we have in stock, what we are working with today.

We learned most of the attitudes and beliefs we act on today when we were children. Like biological computers, we churn out the actions of today based on information input years ago. We need to re-program ourselves to operate in today's reality, using appropriate emotions and attitudes and rejecting the old stuff we were given as children.

There are many different ways to do Step Four. Fourth-Step guides are available at many bookstores, especially recovery and self-help bookstores, and there are no membership requirements to shop there.

Here are two suggested approaches to writing an inventory:

Option one is to write an inventory similar to what is done in Alcoholics Anonymous. (See the "Big Book." *Alcoholics Anonymous World Services, Inc.,* New York, ©1976, p. 65.) Take a sheet of paper and divide it into three columns. Label these columns: *Who; Why I'm Angry/Resentful; What It Affects.*

In the first column, we list people that we resent or with whom we are angry. These might include our abuser, our parents, our spouse or significant other, our boss; anyone with whom we are angry right now—write down whoever pops into your mind. Whether it is someone in our lives right now, or the kid that lived down the street when we were 10, we write it down.

In the second column, next to their names, we write down the reasons why we are angry at each person. If it is our perpetrator, the reason most likely will be that they abused us. Probably there will be other reasons; we can be angry at one person for many different reasons. Maybe we resent our spouse for flirting with someone else at a party. Maybe the boss made a snide remark about us during a meeting. Whatever the reasons are, we write them down in the second column.

In the third column, we write down what aspects of our lives have been affected by this resentment/anger. The flirting may have affected our sex life, our pride, and our self-esteem. The snide remark might have affected our pride, self-esteem, job relations. The incest affected our self-esteem, our pride, our boundaries, our sex life, our ability to trust—this particular list can go on and on.

The basic underlying emotion in all of this is fear. Without realizing it, most of our lives have been dominated by fear. We've been afraid that someone will abuse us again, or that someone will discover we aren't as *together* as we try to make it seem. Or we're afraid our significant other will leave us, or that we'll look stupid in front of others. As we begin to recognize these patterns, we can begin to change these automatic responses.

After we have written this resentment/anger list, we write a fear inventory of everything we are afraid of, perhaps starting with *being abused,* and including *heights* and *snakes.* As we begin to trust our Higher Power and confront issues instead of running from them, all of these fears will begin to fade.

Next, we write a sex inventory. We include in this list the things that were done to us, and the things that we did to or with others. We ask our Higher Power to direct our thinking and actions into sane, rational channels with regard to sex. Our abuse has left us with distorted views of sex. Perhaps we seek out inappropriate sexual encounters, or we never have sexual feelings, even when they are appropriate. What we are hoping to find is moderation in such extreme opposites, leading to a healthy sex life and a healthy life in general.

Another method of writing an inventory is to write the story of our lives. (First suggested by Bill B. in his book,

Compulsive Overeater, CompCare Publications, Minneapolis, Minnesota, ©1981, p. 60-63.)

We begin with a prenatal inventory, then divide our lives into major age groupings and write the history of each segment.

In the prenatal inventory, we write a short story about what it felt like while we were still in the womb. We imagine the feelings and attitudes of the people around us and how they affected us. If our mother tried to abort us, or frequently said or implied she wished we had never been conceived, that is a form of abuse.

> **Serena said:** My family didn't want me to be born. My mother frequently complained about "that damned second shift" and how the disruption in their schedule caused the pregnancy. My brother hated the idea that he would no longer be the youngest, the special child. **From these attitudes, Serena learned resentment, jealousy, abandonment and shame. Her reactions to these feelings shaped her life.**

We write down how we felt, even during birth itself. Most of this will be a fantasy, but it will reflect how we feel about others and ourselves right now. Our character defects will begin to show up in this writing without our even being aware of them.

Next we write a short history of what life was like for us between the ages of 0 and 5. We write down who did what to us, and the emotions and attitudes people expressed toward us. Maybe in all of this we won't have conscious memories, but our inner child will remember, and will help us to identify these things. Or, we can make this up too, maybe from comments we've heard our families make or attitudes we notice now. This part of our inventory will likely consist mostly of what was done to us, because at this age we didn't know right from wrong, and we were being acted upon.

Then we write about ages 5 to 12 and what happened then. It is here that we will begin to write of things we did to harm others. Most of the character defects reflected here will be those we learned from other people's examples. And as we write of the important people and events in our lives during this period, we look for any situations that were important to us—not only the sexual abuse-related issues. This is a searching inventory—we investigate every aspect of our lives as thoroughly as possible.

Then we do the same thing for ages 12 to 20, 20 to 30, 30 to 40, etc., until we reach our current age.

Gradually we recognize that the actions and attitudes of the people around us when we were tiny are the actions and attitudes we have internalized and used as we've gotten older. We are reacting to situations today with the same attitudes that we used when we were 4 years old. For those of us abused at an older age, the abuse changed and colored our attitudes, but for the most part we are what we were taught as children. We are also acting and reacting just the way our families did.

Is this the way we want to live now? Do we want to keep letting history dictate our actions, or do we want to start living in today's reality?

Many victims of sexual abuse can't remember much of their childhood, especially the periods related to the trauma. For us, it may be helpful to do our inventory in reverse order, starting with our present age and going backward in increments of 10 years, until we come to the place where we cannot remember. The mind is kind and nothing more than we can handle will be revealed to us. We just start our inventory in the manner with which we are most comfortable.

The other important point to this inventory is that we *finish* it. Not finishing it gives us a good reason not to feel any more pain. It allows us to avoid the pain of sharing our inventory with another human being. To continue our journey of recovery, we must finish this inventory. It may not be perfect. It may not be "absolutely everything that ever happened in my entire life," but that's okay. We finish it, so we can move on, and we give ourselves credit for what we have been able to do. When we get to Step Ten, we will take care of any loose ends not covered here.

This Step takes courage. It is very courageous to reveal everything that we've never told anyone before. It's very scary to look into our past this deeply. It can be overwhelming, but fear is one of the character defects that we are going to outgrow.

> **Marianne told us:** After doing my Step Four, I was looking for some surge of great emotional feeling. Instead, I was so calm. My whole entire life was in black and white on these pages of paper. I realized I could not change the history on these pages, but I could change my reactions in my present day situations. I did not see any criticism or judgments on these pages, just a list of facts that were so very true. I still can't believe how calming this inventory was for me. Is this what serenity is? I also knew there were more Steps to do, and the calm reduced my fears and gave me the courage to continue with my recovery.

The courage we gain from writing this inventory will help us face other frightening things that happen to us. We need to start this inventory, and we need to finish it. Our Higher Power will give us the courage to do just that.

Step Four Questions

▸ Are you angry at your abuser?

▸ Are you angry at yourself?

▸ Do you resent your abuser for stealing your life?

▸ Are you angry at other people for not protecting you from the abuse?

▶ Do you feel anger toward everyone around you?

▶ Do you not feel any anger—even about being abused—or are you numb most of the time?

▶ Have you set any boundaries, whether physical, emotional or spiritual, to ensure your safety?

▶ Do you permit yourself to change boundaries as necessary?

▶ Are you afraid to experience sexual arousal?

▶ Do you hate or fear people of the opposite sex?

▶ Do you hate or fear people of the same sex?

▶ Do you seek out inappropriate sexual encounters?

▶ Do you find that you cannot have a loving relationship with anyone?

▶ Do you feel like you have an extra-heavy burden to carry that other people don't?

▶ Are you afraid to trust anyone?

▶ Are you afraid to trust yourself?

▶Do you get upset when you hear that things will be done differently than you are accustomed to?

▶ Are you afraid to feel your anger because you feel like you will explode if you let any anger out?

▶ Are you afraid of people who remind you of those who abused you?

▶ Do sudden movements or loud noises frighten you?

▶ Do you need to remain constantly aware of the people and movement around you?

▶ Are you afraid to let anyone see the real you?

▶ Are you afraid to tap into blocked memories because you don't think you can live through the pain?

▶ Do you feel like garbage as a result of your abuse?

► Have you abandoned yourself as one person and become many in order to deal with the hurt?

► Do you feel alone all the time?

► Do you run away when you find someone getting too close for comfort?

► Do you find yourself running away from you?

► Do you find yourself reliving past experiences as though they were happening today?

► Are you responding to a situation today as though you were a child with no control over your life?

► Do you believe that you have choices in your life today?

► Do you find yourself losing hours out of your day, with no memory of what happened?

► Do you dissociate from reality if you feel threatened?

► If everything is going well, do you worry and wait for the bad things to happen again?

► Have you given yourself permission to take the time necessary to grieve your losses and pain?

► If your memories have just surfaced, have you taken the time to grieve the years you spent in denial?

► Do you believe that nobody could possibly have had a worse life than you?

► Do you play "poor me" or "can you top this" when you talk with others?

► If you have multiple personalities, can you acknowledge that these *parts* hold the key to finding some of the answers to what happened in your life?

► Have you accepted responsibility for your life?

► Have you begun standing up for your rights?

► Are you punishing yourself by smoking, or by using alcohol, or some other mind-altering chemicals to numb out?

▸ Do you need the thrill of gambling, or spending too much, to feel alive?

▸ Do you need to cut or mutilate yourself to let out some of the enormous pain?

▸ Have you written down what you feel shame for?

▸ Do you feel shame when you make a mistake?

▸ Are you keeping secrets that should be shared?

▸ Did your abuser threaten to hurt you if you told the secrets?

Authors' Note: We don't believe it is ever necessary to forgive others or to confront anyone. The Twelve Steps don't ever mention forgiveness or confrontation. The choice to forgive or to confront should be left to each individual. Some will feel forgiveness or confrontation is necessary, others won't.

▸ Do you feel you need to forgive the people that hurt you in order to progress in your recovery?

▸ Do you feel that you can never forgive those people?

▸ Have you made a decision to confront your abuser?

▸ What do you hope to gain by this confrontation: money, love, support, an apology?

▸ Will these things deny or invalidate your memories?

▸ Will you be able to accept whatever happens?

▸ Are you willing to give yourself time to get in touch with your true feelings about forgiveness and confrontation?

▸ Can you use your energy to address the issues of incest, sexual abuse, or rape, instead of attacking your abuser?

▸ If you are an adult, can you look at yourself and accept that the abuser cannot control your life anymore unless you permit it?

Step Five

We admitted to our Higher Power, to ourselves and to another human being the exact nature of our wrongs.

Step Five

Having completed our Fourth-Step Inventory to the best of our ability at this time, we need to admit our wrongs to our Higher Power, to ourselves, and to another person. We need to acknowledge where we are wrong before we can begin to make changes. This will take honesty and courage—it can be very difficult to admit to anyone what was done to us and, more importantly, what we have done to others.

We admit to our Higher Power what has happened to us and what we have done to ourselves and to others. We remember our new loving relationship with our Higher Power and we trust that our Higher Power always loves us. Giving our Fourth Step over to our Higher Power will prepare us to tell another human being.

Some people feel that the act of writing the inventory is an effective way of telling our Higher Power. Others have a conversation with their Higher Power, revealing what happened in their lives. As we have been comforted by our Higher Power as we have worked through our inventory, so will we find non-judgmental compassion and love as we relate our story of abuse. Our Higher Power has always known our sufferings, and will listen without condemning and with complete attention. As we grow closer and closer to our Higher Power, we will believe that we are not judged or condemned because we were sexually used and abused.

Having told our Higher Power our complete moral inventory, we are now ready to tell ourselves the truth. Admitting the truth to ourselves, maybe for the first time with our walls of denial down, will give us a new perspective on ourselves. We can see the patterns we have developed that have kept us in a victim role. We'll find flaws in our thought patterns that have held back our maturing process. We will also find potentials that have gone undeveloped because of our insecurities. We will see ourselves in a new spiritual light—as complete individuals with ideas, problems, motivations, and with room for growth.

> **For Shelley, abused by her father for years, writing her inventory finally enabled her to admit to herself the entire truth about her abuse and its long-term effects:** For years I thought that once the abuse finally stopped, it was all over. I thought it had no effect on me whatsoever now that the physical aspect was over. When I did my inventory, I realized that the abuse had affected every single aspect of my life. The patterns of survival I had been using were no longer effective, and in fact were causing me to hurt others. When I admitted these patterns and behaviors, I was able to begin the process of changing them.

We might ask why we have to admit anything to ourselves or our Higher Power, since both know everything anyway. That might very well be true; however, many people we've talked with have said that they hadn't admitted the full truth, even to themselves. They had qualified it, or minimized it, or denied it completely. Remember that knowing the whole truth is the only way to be set free. Only in admitting our brokenness can we find the way to wholeness. Now is the time to be totally honest with our Higher Power and with ourselves about everything.

Mary told us: When my children were little, if they did something wrong or were naughty, I would give them a smack anywhere I could reach on their bodies. I had resolved that I would never spank or beat my children the way I had been, so I thought that one good smack would take care of it. In my insanity, I took it to extremes. I remember one time my 4-year-old daughter ran from me and was cowering in a corner, and I chased her and smacked her so hard her nose bled. Fortunately, I soon realized that even "a good smack" was wrong and changed my behavior. But I had never thought this was abuse until I was doing my inventory and had to admit this to my Higher Power and to myself. It was one of the most painful things I had to admit, that I had abused my children physically.

Now that we have shared this inventory with our Higher Power and ourselves, we are prepared to tell another human being everything. This can be the most difficult part of this Step. We have never wanted anyone to know us totally and completely. We have spent most of our adult lives hiding from ourselves in lonely dark corners of our minds. Telling another person will help us to come out of our shell. The secrets which we were told to keep forever are not our secrets; they were given to us by sick, hurting people. As part and parcel of Step Five, we must cleanse our memories of these secrets.

It takes courage, honesty and humility to tell someone else what we've just begun to face ourselves.

Noelle was afraid to finish Step Five. She had been ridiculed and told she was lying when she was young and tried to tell her parents about what her teacher had done. She said: Telling God is one thing, because what's God going to do, hurl a lightning bolt at me or drop me through a crack in the earth? But another person, they can laugh at you, they can be embarrassed, they can condemn you, or worst of all, they can desert you.

This is why it is important to find someone we can trust absolutely, someone with whom we feel totally safe. They must understand that this information is confidential, never to be talked about or gossiped about with others.

We try to choose wisely the individual with whom we will complete Step Five. We might ask members of a Twelve-Step program which person they felt comfortable enough with to share their inventory. If we have strong ties to a religious denomination, we might consider telling the leader of that group. We might choose a therapist with whom we have developed a trusting relationship—or a family member, a close friend, or our Twelve-Step program sponsor.

Remember, we are going to tell this person everything. If one of the things that we have to admit is that we have been unfaithful to our spouse, we should not choose our spouse as the person to whom we will admit these things. We search for someone who will understand why we are doing this. We aren't looking for sympathy or approval. We need to be heard—maybe for the first time—and perhaps gain some insights into our actions and reactions. We aren't on a witch hunt and we aren't crying for pity. We need to talk honestly about all of our wrongs and get them straight in our minds so that we can begin to change and heal.

> **Frederica chose a member of her sexual abuse survivors group to be the one to tell:** I felt that no one "out there" could possibly understand what had happened to me, and what I had done as a result of the abuse, unless they had been through similar experiences themselves. I didn't feel safe telling just anyone about my mother's "little parties." It had to be someone who would believe me and would be able to help me find some direction and meaning in my life. My friend in the group fit the bill completely. She understood about confidentiality, and also knew that I had to do this for my sanity and peace of mind.

It is usually helpful to begin this Step shortly after finishing an inventory. When we come together with the person we have chosen, we share everything that we have written with them. We don't try to hide anything. This is the beginning of a cleansing process that will spark a change in our lives. We are totally honest and open; first we tell this person what was done to us, then we tell them what we have done to others. Our inventory has been written to discover our defects. Although the sexual abuse was not our wrong, we accept responsibility for our actions when we *have* been wrong.

The way we have carried the effects of our abuse into our own behavior is our responsibility. If sarcasm has been one of our survival techniques, then we need to look at those we might have hurt with it. Perhaps we have become compulsive spenders or gamblers, we must look at what harm we may have caused by using our money in these negative ways. If lying has been our instinctive reaction to many situations, where have we hurt others by lying? Now is the time to put away self-pity, denial, self-righteousness and grandiosity, and be totally honest about our entire lives.

Other new feelings and memories might surface while we are giving away our Fifth Step. If they do, we discuss them as another part of Step Five. In order to recover, it is important to admit everything to the person we have chosen—even the absolute worst things we can remember. When we tell someone everything, we share our burden; we open the dark corridors of the past and shed some light on our deepest secrets. We have been hiding behind our masks and using dysfunctional survival tools for too long. Now is the time to unmask our true selves, and let someone else know us for who we really are. Let someone else see the hurt, the pain, the guilt, the shame, and the distorted view of the world given to us by our perpetrators.

Every abuse victim we talked with said that they have always felt different than other people, and that they didn't fit in anywhere. We have been living in solitude too long. We've spent a lot of time and energy isolating ourselves from the world so we couldn't and wouldn't be hurt anymore. When we share our life history with someone else, we find that we aren't alone anymore; we feel a kinship with another person. We finally have no more secrets to keep. A tremendous burden is lifted. Now it is time to rejoin the human race. We can choose to be alone, but we don't have to be lonely anymore. And it's wonderful to know that someone else finally knows the truth and believes us.

Sharing our inner thoughts and feelings with another person will help us to overcome the toxic shame we took away from the abuse. It will give us a new freedom as a recovered individual with our inner self and our inner child acknowledged for the first time. It will help to clear out the residue of guilt, condemnation and humiliation that was used to control us when we were being abused.

It may feel shameful and degrading to tell someone all of the things we have done. That is okay. We will draw strength from our Higher Power to do this. When we are finished, we will no longer be standing alone as we seem to have done all our lives. This will be the beginning of true humility, admitting our strengths and our weaknesses. Sharing helps us see that we are people that deserve to be heard, and who have something worthwhile to say. Admitting our faults and flaws out loud will help us to hear the words that we have written. This will give us a more complete feeling of ourselves. It will also add more weight to what we have felt. As we speak, we may find answers to questions that we dared not ask before. It is a freeing experience to finally admit everything, to begin to let it go, and to turn it over to that force beyond ourselves. We may feel a great sense of relief or a sense of lightness. We may feel nothing at all. Working and living the Twelve Steps is a process, not an event or an isolated incident. We are beginning to believe in this healing process. We accept that we are making spiritual progress, and not seeking spiritual perfection.

When we are sharing our inventory, we write down the defects we discover so that we can see exactly what we'll have to change later. The inventory will also serve as a guide for Step Eight, when we make a list of all persons we have harmed.

John, who had been abused by his father until he was 13, did his Step Five with his sponsor: We met at his house and went through everything. I asked my sponsor to write down what defects he heard, and I wrote down the ones I recognized. After I was finished, we compared lists. We had both written down many of the same things. There were a couple that he heard that I hadn't even noticed, so it was really helpful to get his input. We also made a list for my Eighth Step that same night because I didn't want to keep my inventory lying around where someone not so trustworthy might find it. After we had finished, I ripped up my Fourth Step and threw it away. I felt more free than I ever had before.

Feeling free is just one of the benefits we get from doing Step Five. This is a wonderful opportunity to get clarification and feedback about some things that might have puzzled us before. Many times we're not aware that what we are doing is not healthy behavior, even though it is normal behavior for someone who has been sexually abused. Someone who loves and understands us, yet is unassociated with our pain, can help us to see things differently.

Working Step Five is also a great reality check.

Sue, who finally got the courage to leave her husband after 3 years of abuse in their marriage, shared her inventory and was surprised when her sponsor told her that some of the things for which Sue was blaming herself weren't her fault at all: I assumed that everything that happened was my fault. My husband always blamed me for whatever went wrong. He told me that he wouldn't have to beat me or rape me if I had just done something differently. My sponsor helped me to understand that these were lies, that I wasn't at fault. Just because bad things were done to me did not make me a bad person. Because I made a mistake, that doesn't make me a mistake.

After working Step Five, many people begin to feel a sense of forgiveness, both of themselves and of others. So many of us have blamed ourselves for everything that ever happened in our lives. Now is the time to realize we haven't been at fault in everything, and to begin to forgive ourselves when we have been wrong.

It is also a time when we begin to forgive others. This might seem impossible at first. How could anyone ever forgive the abuser in their lives?

Sherrie had been abused by her parents for many years, and went into a rage whenever someone suggested to her that she might forgive them: My close friend and I were arguing about this one day when she said that if I would just use the dictionary definition, I wouldn't be so upset. So I looked it up, and I did calm down. It meant to give up resentment against or the desire to punish someone. I always thought it meant to treat someone as if nothing had happened. When I realized that I would be the one who benefited from forgiveness, not my parents, then I could forgive. Not necessarily forget, but forgive.

Eventually, we will come to an understanding and an acceptance that those people were sick, not just the perpetrators but many of the other people who harmed us throughout our lives. They were sick, warped people who did a lot of harm. They were hurt people who hurt other people. We may only be able at first to see these sick individuals with a little compassion. In time, we may see that our perpetrators acted out as they, in turn, were taught or were acted upon. They may have been passing on their legacy of shame and guilt, as a way of denying their own pain. It is probably hard to believe now, but eventually we may even forgive our abusers.

If we knew someone had cancer and was raging and hurtful, we would understand and pity them because they were sick and couldn't help it. We begin to understand the wrongdoers in our lives—they also had a cancer, a sickness, and their lashing out did us harm.

Perhaps, in the end, the only reason we will find to forgive people will be that our rage, anger and resentment are holding us back from living our lives completely. When we can begin to understand that, then we can begin to heal.

We may choose not to forgive the abusers in our lives. We may never be ready to take that step. That is okay. This is a decision that each individual must make. Nobody can tell us what we *should* or *ought* to do.

At this point in our recovery, we will not let anything or anyone stand between us and recovery. We have written down all our shortcomings and have discussed them with another person. Having purged our mind of all its secrets, we are ready to begin the next step in our healing.

Step Five Questions

➤ Are you afraid that your Higher Power may leave you if you reveal the exact nature of your wrongs?

➤ Do you believe your Higher Power will condemn you for your past?

➤ Do you believe that your Higher Power already knows your weaknesses and unmanageability?

➤ Do you believe that you must keep holding on to this information?

➤ Are you tired of carrying this burden?

➤ How does it feel to admit the truth to your Higher Power?

➤ When you admit your wrongs, are you using your Fourth Step Inventory as a guide?

▶ Will you allow your Higher Power to guide you as you prepare to admit the truth to yourself?

▶ Do you resent having to face and admit the truth to yourself?

▶ Do you feel that you have already gone through too much?

▶ Does this feel like just another burden to bear?

▶ Have you been hiding the truth from yourself by minimizing, denying, blocking, etc.?

▶ Do you believe that now is the time to stop running from yourself?

▶ Can you admit that you have made mistakes?

▶ Are you able to see the patterns that developed in your life?

▶ Can you think of ways to change and improve your old patterns?

▶ Can you admit that you have learned negative behaviors from being abused?

▶ Are you ready to accept responsibility for your acts?

▶ Have you thought carefully about the person with whom you will share this information?

▶ Is there someone you can trust to keep this information safe?

▶ If you have chosen someone, have you been as honest as possible in admitting your wrongs?

▶ Are you willing to let someone see your past exactly as it was?

▶ Are you willing to listen to their suggestions, questions and input?

▶ If you become aware of something not written in your Fourth-Step Inventory, will you share it?

▶ Can you accept the feelings you might have after you have admitted your wrongs to another person?

▶ Can you accept that you might not feel any different after sharing your inventory?

▶ Are you getting rid of the guilt and shame you've carried for so long?

▶ Are you beginning to accept that you are a worthwhile person?

▶ As you shared your inventory, did you write down the character defects you found?

▶ Are you willing to admit that some of your past actions were the result of being abused?

▶ Are you ready to change?

▶ Are you ready to forgive yourself?

▶ Have you thought about forgiving others?

NOTES

Step Six

*We were entirely ready to have our Higher Power
remove all these defects of character.*

Step Six

Step Six continues the changes we began making in Steps Three and Four when we turned our will and our lives over to the care of the Higher Power of our understanding. Our healing is moving ahead without our having to work so hard to force changes. Our Higher Power is doing for us what we have not been able to do for ourselves. We have stopped giving our Higher Power a wish list of projects to complete and change. We are starting to rely on our new faith and trust in a personal Higher Power to enable us to handle new situations that we used to find fearful or difficult. Our lives will become less confusing and have more purpose.

Now that we've written our fearless moral inventory, and shared it with someone else, we need to do something about our shortcomings. We know what behaviors and attitudes we need to change. We've talked about the past and decided that it's time to stop living there. The techniques we have used to survive are now standing in the way of our recovery. We have been preparing ourselves for change by working through the first five Steps.

We now ask ourselves if we really want to change? Do we really want to become a capable individual? Do we really want to remove our faults and negative attitudes? We will take the time while doing Step Six to get ready to let go of these, and to reflect on what these changes can and will mean in our lives.

Step Six is like setting a dinner table before the meal is actually served. We wouldn't serve dinner if we hadn't prepared the table first, so don't jump ahead and ask that these character defects be removed immediately. We can use this preparation time wisely and heal in our Higher Power's time frame, or we can rush through this Step only to have to come back and give ourselves the time needed to heal.

If we find ourselves grieving, we allow ourselves sufficient time for it. For some of us, this Step will be a necessary rest period to become more comfortable with and more confident about the new person we are becoming. Others of us will want to begin immediately after finishing our Step Five. The world around us changes constantly, and we must forge ahead at any and all cost. Instant healing would be too much change for us at one time. It would leave us with too many empty holes to fill. So whatever amount of time is right for you, take it. The important thing is to keep going on your journey into recovery.

We think back over the Steps that we've done so far. Have we truly admitted that our lives are unmanageable and that we are powerless? Do we believe that a force beyond ourselves will restore us to sanity and wholeness? Are we now trusting that force with our will and our lives? Have we written as thorough an inventory as possible and shared it with our Higher Power and another person? If we've done our work so far, then the answer should be, "yes, to the best of my ability." This is tremendous progress on the road to recovery. However, if the answer to any of these questions is no, then we need to take the time now to look at the previous Steps in greater depth.

Perhaps we haven't truly decided to trust a Higher Power with our entire lives. Or maybe we haven't defined a Higher Power that encompasses our needs. We must be sure we have been as thorough as possible.

> **Sally said:** I finally realized that what was holding me back was fear. I realized that if I waited until I was *ready*, then I would never move on. I have to keep going through my fear. Being *ready* might never happen, but by taking a risk and relying instead on the power of the Twelve Steps and my Higher Power, I can become *ready*.

This may be the first time in our lives that we have truly understood why we have reacted the way we have in the past. This is what we are familiar and comfortable with; this is our present frame of reference. But just as old shoes are comfortable but not proper attire for a formal ball, our old patterns don't quite fit with our new growth and outlook on life.

This is the beginning of a lifetime job, the beginning of true change in our lives. Whatever our chronological age, we are worth dedicating the rest of our lives to the recovery process, which will make our lives richer and happier than they would have been without it. We can't let the words *character defects* scare us away from this Step. Character defects are merely habits, attitudes, and actions that aren't right for us anymore. Actually, it's good to be able to list them so that we can see where we need to begin changing.

We need help from some force beyond ourselves to remove these defects, because we haven't been able to change much of anything on our own. Many of us have been living very destructively, abusing our bodies with drugs, alcohol or food. We've tried to change many different times. We've sworn off, gone to clinics, moved to new towns, changed lovers and friends, all to no avail. Only with a Higher Power's help will we be able to make lasting changes in our lives, in our actions and reactions, and in our emotions.

> **Marlene shared with us:** For years I did drugs to numb the pain of having been abused. I learned to deaden all my feelings this way. I'd try to quit now and then, but never made it past the first day. When I started working these Steps and asked my Higher Power to take away my obsession, that's the first time I'd ever been able to put down the drugs and leave them. It's been over four years now, and I'm still clean, and still asking my Higher Power's help every day. The pain of my memories has gradually lessened. I feel like I'm finally living.

If we feel like we aren't ready yet to give up our defects, we ask our Higher Power for willingness. Maybe there will be some defects that we just can't give up yet, like lack of trust or fear of strangers. Right now we only need to be "willing to be willing." We have to be willing to say, "maybe someday." The only thing that will cause us problems with this Step is saying, "never." As soon as we close our hearts and minds to the possibility of changing something, we are closing our minds to any Higher Power and to ourselves. We are digging in our heels and saying, "my way is better, and nothing will ever make me change my mind." This is holding on to our own will, not trusting our Higher Power's will, or even wanting to find out what that will is. Sometimes this comes from our child within, who needs to be in complete control of our feelings to feel safe. We need to reassure that child that we are safe now, that our Higher Power will help us do everything we need to do to live safely and sanely.

> **Betsy talked about the various compulsions she had developed as a result of being abused by her brothers:** If I gave up my cigarettes, then I picked up my gum. When I stopped drinking, I started bingeing on junk food. I asked myself, how can I quit everything? How can I just let it all drop? Where is my safety net? These Steps were the answer for me. When I have problems, I ask God to help me be willing to change.

Using our Fourth-Step inventory list, we write down the character defects that need to be removed, and we become willing to release these shortcomings.

We are beginning to experience a new growth. We have taken the time to become detached observers of our lives, to see how our patterns and behaviors have become deeply rooted in our lives. Do we sometimes hear our mother's messages or our father's old tapes playing in our heads? Do we hear the constant chastising and condemning that others did? Perhaps we'll discover that we allow other people to tell us how, when and where to act. We notice how we are acting and reacting in our present situation. If some of these actions are self-destructive behaviors—such as self-inflicted wounds, alcohol abuse, dangerous relationships—these are the first things we ask our Higher Power to remove from our lives. We take care of our physical safety and change the deadly defects first.

So many of us were taught we were worthless, and that we deserved to be abused, that we have continued abusing ourselves long after the sexual abuse stopped. Some of these abuses aren't as obvious as taking a razor blade and cutting ourselves, or finding partners that will beat us up for any mistakes we make. Perhaps we rage at people whenever someone doesn't fulfill our expectations or makes a small mistake. Maybe we condemn people who do not share our moral or ethical values. Maybe we're so lethargic and listless that we don't get out of bed until 3:00 in the afternoon—even when we go to bed at 9:00 the previous night. Maybe we have 6 hour lunches, beginning with a sandwich and continuing all afternoon with candy, chips and ice cream. Negative self-talk is very destructive: belittling ourselves, calling ourselves stupid for making a mistake, constantly berating ourselves, these are all forms of self-abuse.

Dottie shared: I used to live in the *shoulds, coulds, woulds* all the time. It was always, "I should have … if only I could ... I wish I would have ..." Now, when I hear myself saying these negative things, I ask my Higher Power to help me change my thinking. I don't want to put myself down anymore.

Sometimes we love our defects. They help us to survive. They make us feel alive.

> **Sally said:** Sometimes I'd get feeling so sorry for myself that it was like I was wallowing in it. Or when I was raging with anger, I could feel my blood pumping and I felt energized, like I could conquer the world. Pain was the barometer of my existence. The more I hurt, the more alive I was.

Now that we've found the readily obvious defects, it's time to look carefully for the more subtle ones. If we feel that we're better than others, somehow superior, that's pride. Self-pity, that "poor me, I've had it so rough" feeling, is also a form of reverse pride or grandiosity. A lot of us play games like "can you top this," when we compare our miseries with someone else's to see who has the most difficult life.

Some forms of sexual behavior are character defects. One of these is bed hopping, with no feeling for the other person and with no thought of developing a relationship with anyone. Another sexual defect is deliberately withholding sex from our partner, perhaps in retaliation for some offense against us. Anytime we use our sexuality as a weapon, that is an inappropriate way of using power and control—and thus a character defect.

Many of us have the *I wants:* "I want a car, I want new furniture, I want a new coat." In our urgency to be happy, to feel like someone worthwhile, we try to fill our emptiness with things. This is greed: we need to separate our true *needs* from our *wants*.

The Judeo-Christian *seven deadly sins* of pride, anger, sloth, gluttony, lust, greed and envy are useful as a general guide to looking at defects. Each of these *wrongs* has variations, ranging from total unmanageability to minor difficulties. As we go through these Steps, and continue growing and changing, we will find ourselves moving away from the more serious manifestations of these defects, toward more mild displays. They will never go away completely. We can strive toward perfection as a goal, but we should always bear in mind that it's the journey that is important, not reaching the ultimate destination: perfection is impossible to achieve.

A lot of us spend our lives with our inner child in control. We look like adults, but we're really living as though we're still 5, 10, or perhaps 3 years old. Our inner child has never learned to be happy, and is constantly trying to find happiness "out there" somewhere. We are now ready for our Higher Power to show our inner child that we don't need to have it all; with the help of our Higher Power, we can keep the inner child within each of us safe, and give them the peace they've been searching for.

Step Six asks us to begin reaching toward new, exciting goals. Nobody expects us to become saints. Progress is the goal, not perfection. This isn't another excuse to start berating ourselves again, either. If we fall short of our goal, then we try again. This Step is an opportunity to adjust to what has been, accept our past, then go on from there. Gradually our lives will begin to change, our defects will begin to be removed, and we will begin to have peace within ourselves. And, eventually, we will be comfortable with our new selves.

Step Six Questions

▸ What does *entirely ready* mean to you?

▸ Do you need to spend some time becoming entirely ready?

▸ Are you willing to let go of every negative behavior?

▸ Have you found some positive behaviors to fill the gaps?

▸ Do you feel that you need some time to let go?

▸ Have you worked the first five Steps as thoroughly as you can?

▸ Are you ready to start living with a spiritual guide—your Higher Power?

▸ Are you beginning to trust your Higher Power?

▸ Do you feel able to ask that Higher Power for help, strength and guidance?

▸ Do you have a sense of what your character defects are?

▸ Are you willing to let go of all your character defects?

▸ Are you willing to release some character defects, but not all?

▸ Are you resistant to the idea of changing your old behaviors?

▸ What benefits are you still getting from your character defects?

▸ Are you afraid that, if you give up all your character defects, you'll disappear?

▸ Is the thought of revenge or hatred toward your perpetrator so powerful that you don't want to give it up?

▸ Are you beginning to take risks?

▸ Do you feel a lessening of fear?

▸ Have you looked at your survival tools and acknowledged that they were useful for awhile?

▸ Can you be thankful that they helped you to survive?

▸ Are you ready to change them?

▸ Have you found new and better coping skills?

▸ If you ask your Higher Power to take away your anger and resentments, how will that affect your life?

▸ If you ask your Higher Power to remove your greed or gluttony, what new actions will be necessary to live without them?

▸ If you ask your Higher Power to remove your envy or jealousy, can you begin to accept people for who they are, even if they seem to have more than you do?

▸ Are you willing to let go of the past and live in the here and now?

▸ Do you feel like you're beginning to heal the wounds of sexual abuse and incest?

▸ Are you working in your Higher Power's time frame, rather than your own?

▸ Are you stretching yourself enough?

▸ Are you afraid to take any risks at all?

▸ Are you waiting to be *ready*?

▸ Are you trying to be perfect as you work these Steps, or are you admitting your human imperfections?

▸ Are you accepting that you are doing the best you can, each day, knowing that *best* changes day-by-day?

▸ If you aren't ready to give up everything, are you asking your Higher Power for willingness to be ready?

▸ Are you willing to get your strength from that force beyond yourself instead of feeling like you have to be strong and powerful on your own?

▸ Are you willing to be an adult, with your Higher Power's help?

NOTES

Step Seven

We humbly asked our Higher Power to
remove our shortcomings.

Step Seven

Having completed our preparations in Step Six, we now ask our Higher Power to take away our shortcomings. We ask for help to take this enormous step toward lifelong change. Until now, we have been living in fear and shame, running from pain whenever possible—and sometimes when it hasn't been possible. We tried running, only to find we were running away from ourselves. These Steps are giving us the chance to face pain, to realize that, though something may hurt, it will pass, and we will have grown through the process. We can even use the pain to measure our progress. This reaffirms our trust in this process, our way out of the damaging effects caused by sexual abuse.

We think about why we are doing these Steps, about what we hope to gain. For most of us, it's the chance to truly change our lives. We are tired of living like creatures who have no rights, who feel incomplete and even unnecessary. For some, these Steps will be the last chance we give life, the last chance we have to find hope. By coming this far in the Steps, we've begun to revive our long-buried child within. We've begun to see that there is hope, and that we will be able to change and really live.

The first six steps have led us to an awareness of who and what we are today, and what needs to be changed. Now, in Step Seven, we humbly ask our Higher Power to help us begin that necessary change. These are *our* shortcomings we are asking to have removed. We won't be asking our Higher Power to change our parents, or our significant others, or our children or anyone else out there that we think needs changing.

> **Marie told us:** My friends at the meeting told me a new version of an old prayer: "God, grant me the serenity to accept the people I cannot change, courage to change the person I can, and the wisdom to know that that's me." I've used this often to remember whose defects I'm asking to change.

Although we are asking our Higher Power to begin changing us, there is no magic wand to wave over our heads and mysteriously remove all of our defects. There is no fairy dust or moonbeam to cause change; plain and simple hard work is what will do it. We have to work at changing ourselves. Through our Higher Power we can find the strength and courage we need to keep on working and changing.

We will need humility throughout this Step. *Humility* is far different from *humiliation*. They sound the same, and many people use them interchangeably, but there's a big difference.

We've known *humiliation* all our lives. People have shamed us and tried to humiliate us every chance they got. The abusers in our lives certainly contributed shame and humiliation to our lives. Perhaps others—teachers, parents, neighbors and even friends—have added to that feeling of humiliation that we are so imbued with. Sadly enough, we've brought humiliation onto ourselves by setting ourselves up in situations that would embarrass us or hurt us. We don't do this consciously, but it still happens all the time. We've known humiliation; we've gotten comfortable in it, even though it hurts. At least it's a hurt that we're familiar with, and we know how to get through. This sabotaging of ourselves is something else that is going to change as a result of working these Steps.

Humility is knowing ourselves honestly, both the positive and the negative aspects of ourselves. Humility is knowing and being proud of who we are, not in a boastful way, but in a quiet recognition of our self-worth and abilities. Humility gives us the ability to see ourselves in a different light, to look at the parts we have played in other people's lives. Humility is recognizing the less than desirable aspects of ourselves, and making a conscious effort to change those negative aspects into positive ones. Perhaps we had a need to always have the last word in a fight. Or maybe we always needed to prove to others that we were bigger, brighter or better. But we don't need these defenses any longer, so now we ask for them to be removed.

All of the Twelve Steps are a search for humility, a move toward honest self-knowledge and then self-betterment. It took humility to admit that we were powerless and that we needed a power outside ourselves to help us. It took humility to share with someone else our faults, then to ask our Higher Power to remove them.

We've already gotten some release from our pain by using humility. It's a great relief to lay down the burden of trying to run our lives on our own power. Sharing our histories and our defects relieved us of the deadly secretiveness that we've lived with for years. There is nothing shaming about humility. By striving for humility we will become better, healthier people.

Before we used these Steps, we never seemed to have enough: enough things, enough people, enough love. We were constantly trying to fill our emptiness with material possessions or someone else's love. It only served to emphasize and reinforce our already low opinions of ourselves. We felt like the trash and scum of the earth, so why try to change? It never occurred to us that the solution might rest in improving ourselves, and in finding a spiritual base upon which we could live. As we grow through these Steps, our self-esteem is improving; we are accepting that we are worthy people, that we are good, and that we have rights—especially the right to be treated and respected as a human being.

There are a few things we consider in preparation for this process. First, we take into account the faith and trust we have developed in our Higher Power. This is the time to reaffirm our commitment to that spiritual force. We trust in the process and time frame that our Higher Power is using to remove our shortcomings, and that we will not be asked to surrender any more than we can manage at one time. Again, we remember that healing is a process and not an event.

Next, we consider our change from a material-based way of life to a spirituality-based one. Spiritual values come first for us now. We understand that when we rely only on ourselves, we are blocking out the universal force. But now we know we can rely on our Higher Power for strength and guidance in everything, and that this is the pathway to serenity and peace.

We also consider the grieving process as our shortcomings are removed. We don't necessarily like our bad habits, but they have been a part of our make-up for so long that we will miss them. We give ourselves time to grieve and to heal.

> **Patrick shared:** I could slip into my old defects as easily as I could my old jeans and sweatshirt. It was time, though, to throw the old behaviors away, just as I had to throw away my favorite pants when they got too raggedy and torn. It hurt, but I knew that after a few tries, my new stuff would feel just as comfortable as the old.

In this Step, we ask our Higher Power to take away all of our defects of character. We could beg or even dare our

Higher Power to take away our shortcomings. We could expect that force to do the work for us and simply throw our shortcomings away. But this would leave us with a very large hole in our spiritual selves. Just as nature supplies seed and food for all the animals of the earth, but they have to seek out that food, so too do we have to do the foot work, we have to take the action necessary to change.

We will be changing our focus from ourselves and starting to look for ways in which we can be of benefit to others.

> **Diana shared:** I spent my entire life looking out for number one—me. I know now that I have to help others, be aware of others' needs or pain. When I get out of myself and my misery and try to help someone else, my life is easier. It's still a mystery to me why it works that way, but it does. To keep my healing, I had to share it and give it away.

But we don't look for ways to help others in a self-destructive way. Many of us spent our lives focusing on other people and their needs, instead of looking at our own lives. We search for a good balance in this situation, as we look for that same balance in all our circumstances.

Sometimes it's difficult to figure out how to actually do this Step. For some of us, talking with our Higher Power and asking for our difficulties to be removed is enough. Many of us say structured prayers, asking God to remove our shortcomings and acknowledging that we are ready to do God's will, not our own. Some of us will pick a "defect of the day" from our list of character defects, and ask for help in the morning to overcome that defect, being aware throughout the day when opportunities to change that defect come along.

> **Janice shared one imaginative method:** My sponsor told me to blow up an imaginary balloon, and with each breath blow into the balloon all the anger, or shyness, or whatever, that I'm asking my Higher Power to remove. Tie a knot in the balloon, and release the balloon to the

universe. It sounds really simplistic, but it helped me to get a handle on what this Step means.

One shortcoming that many of us share is obsessively thinking about past or future events, worrying about them or replaying them in our minds until we become immobilized. When we find ourselves doing that, we can ask for help to change. Every time we become aware that we're thinking about the situation again, stop and replace the thoughts with thoughts about our spiritual life. We can thank our Higher Power for the strength we've been given to change, or for all the wonderful things we're now able to do. Sometimes we might have to ground ourselves in reality by thinking, "Now I am brushing my teeth; now I am combing my hair."

> **Martha shared:** I've had memories that I just couldn't get out of my mind. I'd see the same things over and over in my mind. I thought I would go crazy. I began asking my god to remove this obsession. There are still some times when I have to ask over and over, but it always works. When I'm sincere and truly mean what I'm saying, the memories fade away.

Looking back over our list of defects, we can write down what the opposite action is for each defect. Perhaps fear is on our list. We write down courage. The opposite of being judgmental is acceptance of others. The opposite of negative self-talk is loving messages to ourselves. For the *seven deadly sins:* the opposite of pride is humility; the opposite of anger is love and forgiveness; the opposite of sloth is action; for gluttony it is discipline; the opposite of lust is sincere regard for the other person; for greed it is generosity; and for envy it is gratitude. When we practice these opposite actions, we can't practice our character defects. We can't be selfish if we are being generous and thinking of others. We can't be critical of others if we are accepting them exactly as they are. This is a great way to keep changing and growing.

This process of change lasts a lifetime, and we will need to continue to ask for help to remove our shortcomings for the rest of our lives. We aren't going to be saints; our defects will always be with us. They just won't have the same intensity as before. We will be able to overcome them gradually, and eventually we will realize that we are acting and reacting differently. Where once we accepted other people's blame for their actions, we will be able to say, "that is not my guilt." Someone that we never could tolerate before will spend some time with us, and several days later we'll realize that we reacted to that person just as we would to anyone about whom we felt neutral. When we realize that we've done something differently, or that we have acted in a totally new and more helpful manner, we will acknowledge that change, congratulate ourselves, and thank our Higher Power for this new behavior. We've always been good at criticizing ourselves. We need to take every opportunity we can to find the good in our actions and praise ourselves. It's our job to rebuild our self-esteem. Noticing and taking pride in our positive growth will help.

> **Edith had been used by her parents and grandparents in their ritualistic ceremonies. She told us:** For the longest time, any change or awareness in my actions was nerve-wracking. My body acted as though I was going to be attacked at any minute. I thought all awareness was awful. Today, I am using awareness as signals that something has changed or must be changed. I can even give myself a pat on the back sometimes. Change is not as scary as it was in the beginning. I have found that Good Orderly Direction [GOD, see page 21] is becoming a daily event in my life. I'm so glad I didn't quit when things seemed to be too difficult.

We realize that some things won't change right away, even if we ask our Higher Power to take the pain or negative behavior away. There will be times when the only action we can take is to do nothing.

Frank, who had been molested by his fourth grade teacher, found this to be very difficult: The hardest thing I've had to learn to do is to just *be*. I always want to take action, to fix it, to change things around, to get relief. I've come to accept that there are times when I need to feel the feelings and just sit with them, or that I have to wait for a solution to come in my Higher Power's time, not mine. Patience doesn't come easily for me, but I'm learning.

Other times we will be able to take action, but we have to remember that most change is gradual; it's a process, not an instant transformation. It is usually a slow process, not a marathon to be run at the fastest pace possible.

Step Seven requires us to practice humility in our daily lives. We continue this practice, even on an hourly basis if that is all we can handle. Doing this will enhance the spiritual growth that we've experienced so far. We will begin to be more observant of others. We will stop being so self-absorbed and we'll be able to participate in life more freely than ever before. Others will begin to like us better. More importantly, we will begin to like ourselves. It's nice when other people like us, but it's ecstasy when we can look in the mirror and honestly say, "Self, I love you, just as you are today."

Step Seven Questions

▸ Do you understand the difference between humility and humiliation?

▸ Are you beginning to recognize your negative attitudes and behaviors?

▸ What steps are you taking to change these shortcomings?

▸ When opportunities to practice new behaviors arise, do you take them?

▸ Can you ask your Higher Power for help in making those changes?

▶ Can you acknowledge your strengths as well as your weaknesses?

▶ Are you willing to feel the pain, knowing that you will feel a serenity and peace later?

▶ Are you ready to acknowledge your rights and responsibilities?

▶ Is your self-esteem beginning to improve?

▶ Are you beginning to recognize that you are a worthwhile human being?

▶ Are you asking your Higher Power to relieve you of the expectations of others?

▶ Are you honestly and sincerely asking your Higher Power to remove your shortcomings?

▶ Are you asking your Higher Power for balance in your life?

▶ What methods are you using to ask your Higher Power to remove your shortcomings?

▶ Are they working?

▶ Are you still worrying about past events?

▶ Do you replay the negative thoughts over and over in your head?

▶ Do you still rehearse for tomorrow? or the next day? or next week?

▶ Are you able to do the footwork, and leave the results to your Higher Power?

▶ Have you tried doing the opposite of your character defects?

▶ When you notice changes, do you take the time to celebrate them?

▶ When you do things differently, does that give you courage to continue?

▶ Are you beginning to take pride in yourself?

▸ Are you demanding that your Higher Power do things when and how you want them done?

▸ Are you starting to like yourself more?

▸ Do you feel a sense of freedom?

▸ Are other people seeing changes in you?

Step Eight

*We made a list of all persons we had harmed, and
became willing to make amends to them all.*

Step Eight

Step Eight calls for more action. We are going to continue the work we began in Steps Four and Five. Perhaps we wrote this amends list at the same time we shared our Step Five. If not, now is the time to write it. The timing isn't all that important—what counts is thoroughness and honesty.

Using our Fourth-Step Inventory, we prepare a list of people whom we have harmed. This includes everyone we know that we have injured in any way. This is part of the process of cleaning up our past; it will enable us to get on with our new lives of sanity and peace, seeking to do our Higher Power's will and helping others to the best of our abilities. We will write our list now, and through the rest of our lives we will be adding names as we recognize others that we've harmed, and crossing out names as we finish our amends. We will be honest and responsible in making our list, because this will be the beginning of the end of our isolation from others. When we don't have to worry about the past, and we know the hurts of the past are healed, we are better able to fill our lives with new and wholesome relationships.

Most of us start this list with ourselves. We are the most important person in our lives and the one we have harmed the most. Many of us have abused ourselves far more than we ever hurt others, or were hurt by others. We have judged ourselves very harshly, and always in a very negative light. By putting our own name at the head of our list, we offer ourselves the same amends we extend to the other people we have harmed. We can't become ready to make amends to anyone else if we can't make amends to ourselves first.

For some of us, continuing to hurt ourselves after the actual abuse ended seemed like the natural thing to do. To help us cope with our lives and our negative feelings, we turned to anything that would stop the pain—drugs, self-mutilation, diet abuse—yet it continued to sabotage our efforts to live normally.

Some of us tortured our minds with sickness, or we developed multiple personalities to hide our memories. Maybe we became what someone else wanted us to be, or maybe we denied our very existence as a complete and separate individual with wants, needs, feelings and emotions of our own.

We need to change these behaviors and begin to make amends to ourselves. These survival methods are inappropriate and not in harmony with the new persons we are becoming. We are slowly getting to know ourselves and to have new ideas and goals that are surfacing in our healing process. We cannot continue to live in the past and have our tomorrows stolen from us because we are beating ourselves up with shame and guilt. We must live in today, and forgive ourselves for the past.

As survivors, many of us write our amends list with the help of a sponsor, or other trustworthy individual, who can help us look at various situations in our lives honestly. Because we've been victims, it's easy for us to deny or minimize our responsibility for anything we've done. Sometimes we get so wrapped up in being the victim that we can't see where we've harmed anyone.

Yvette had been emotionally abandoned by her mother as well as abused by her father. To compensate, she tried to give her own family what she had lacked in her family of origin: I've been so abused, I thought I would never hurt anyone else. I've been kind and done the opposite of what was done to me all my life. In fact, I went completely overboard the other way. I gave everything to my spouse and children, while I lost myself in the process. I paid a very high price, but I also robbed my family of the opportunity to experience the hard knocks of life and didn't allow them to learn the necessary coping skills so they would not be victims in other ways themselves.

We might feel that we've never harmed anyone at all. However, it's practically impossible to be alive and not harm someone. Maybe we didn't kill anyone or abuse anyone, but there are many ways to hurt others, sometimes without even realizing it.

Some of us become so over-protective of our children that, rather than risk having them be hurt the way we were, we stifle their natural curiosity and creativity. Many things in life are painful. We need to be aware of the real dangers, but it isn't possible to protect anyone—ourselves or our children—from all of life's pain. And we can drive ourselves crazy trying to.

Often, in our efforts to help our loved ones, we *enable* them to continue their own harmful behaviors by stepping in to rescue them from themselves. For instance, when we call in sick for an alcoholic spouse—covering for the latest in a string of all-night drinking binges—or when we give money to someone we know is going to gamble, drink or snort it away, and who will never pay it back, we are helping these people avoid facing their dysfunctions. Everyone needs to be allowed to make their own mistakes and to deal with their own consequences.

Perhaps we deprive someone of our love because we are afraid to have anyone love us? Perhaps we start fights so we can believe other people only mean us harm? Does our fear of abandonment lead us to build huge imaginary walls to keep people away from us? Maybe we try in every possible way to please everyone else, and lose ourselves in the process. Such behaviors hurt them and us—nobody wins. All these people need to go on our list.

For the rest of the list, we will be looking at where we have been harmful to others, not where they have harmed us. We need to include absolutely anyone we can remember that we have harmed. This can include family members, friends, businesses, acquaintances, employers, almost anyone we've come in contact with throughout our lives.

Some of us have asked, "Do I have to include everyone, even people that I'll never see again or who are dead?" The answer is an emphatic yes! At this point we are only writing down names. Nobody is asking us to actually go out there and make amends yet. That's in the next Step. We have spent our lives either running from our problems or refusing to be accountable for our actions and reactions. Now, we are being asked to slow down our lives and stay in the present simply by making a list and not projecting or worrying about what comes next.

Right now, all we're concerned with is honesty and thoroughness. We look back through our lives and accept our responsibility for our actions. We acknowledge where we have been wronged and how this wrong has caused us to hurt others and ourselves.

One very important thing we have to remember is that we are *not* responsible for whatever abuse we suffered, no matter what our age at that time.

> **Frankie shared:** My counselor kept telling me to forget about who did what to me, that what I needed to do was accept my responsibility for the abuse. But [that counselor was wrong], through working these Steps and through the help of other survivors, I have been able to

understand that *I had no responsibility for my abuse.* I didn't ask to be raped when I was six. I didn't ask to be forced to have oral sex with my father. I was abused, and that is his responsibility, not mine.

When we write this list, we mustn't fall into the habit of blaming ourselves for everything that ever happened. This is easy for us to do, since many of us took on the role of scapegoat in our families of origin. To try to keep peace, we accepted the blame for everything, whether or not we were actually responsible. We must learn to accept responsibility for our part, but we aren't totally at fault in everything. This list is not an excuse to further batter ourselves.

Some of us were given the message that we were bad—everything we did was terrible. Throughout our lives, we have continued to give ourselves this message. We have ignored any compliments we received, deserved or not. We have criticized ourselves, called ourselves names and generally put ourselves down. This isn't necessary any longer. We may have made some mistakes, but that doesn't make us bad people; mistakes do not make us a mistake, only imperfect human beings like everyone else. As we strive to grow in our new lives, it is important to realize that we've perpetuated our perpetrators' negative messages to us. And as we continue to work these Steps, we can cancel out our old harmful messages and replace them with new, loving, nurturing ones.

In this Step, we honestly evaluate our relationships and determine where we've been at fault, and where we need to make amends for our wrongs. We need not make all the amends now, we just write everything down.

Jocelyn, whose stepfather abused her repeatedly, told us: When I was making my list with my sponsor, there were a few people that I wasn't sure if I had harmed or not. At the time, I felt that I had been more wronged by them. She suggested I write them down anyway for future consideration. Sure enough, after a couple of years of working through the Steps and continuing with my recovery, I decided that I did owe those people amends.

Some of us have found it easier to start by reviewing our relationships with our family members first. We look at how we have hurt them. It seems reasonable that we've probably harmed those closest to us, because we spend more time with them, and it's usually safer to reveal ourselves with all our faults to someone close to us.

Did we unfairly vent our anger at someone else onto our spouse or significant other because they were safer? Sometimes we "grin and bear it" when we feel humiliated in public, then go home and rage against our kids or other family members. Maybe we criticized and ridiculed our siblings for being too fat, or too stupid, or for something else. It's time to realize that we hurt them by our actions and our name-calling. Maybe we really believed they were "airheads" or maybe we thought we were being helpful to point out they were eating far too much, but we are learning now that they don't have to meet our standards any more than we have to meet other people's. No one said we were in charge or that everyone else had to meet our expectations.

It's all too easy to be judgmental or critical of others; that way we don't have to face our own issues. We can spend our time focusing on others and their problems. Even if they don't think they have problems, we're always happy to point their errors out to them. However, this is a personal program and we must not use these Steps to try to change anyone but ourselves.

Friends probably come next on our list of amends. Maybe we expect them to always understand our problems, to always be there whenever we need them, to always support and love us. This would be wonderful, but it isn't possible in real life. Our friends have other commitments, other people in their lives, just as we do. Nobody can always be there for someone else. Only our Higher Power is able to be continually on our side—*always* there for us. If we have demonstrated anger or hurt about this to our friends, they go on the amends list. Some of us continually test our friendships, seeing just how much our friends will put up with, so that eventually the test is too difficult and we can say, "See, I told you that person didn't really like me. I always end up with lousy friends. It just isn't fair." We try to control and bend others to meet our expectations. We demand that others do as we want them to, and when it doesn't work, we blame them. Now it's time to realize what we've been doing, and when we've harmed others by these actions, we put those names on our list.

We might need to list some businesses. Many of us stole candy or magazines from the local store, or shoplifted a sweater when our friends dared us. Some of us have padded our expense accounts, rationalizing that everyone does it. Perhaps we stole money from the petty cash fund, or *borrowed* scissors, a ream of paper, envelopes or paper clips. We think about our work habits. Do we give a full day's work for a full day's pay? Do we make 20-minute personal phone calls, perhaps long distance, on the company phone; or take an hour-and-a-half lunch, when we're only scheduled to have 45 minutes. This is in fact stealing our employer's time, money and inventory. It is doing harm to others, and we need to make amends for these wrongs.

We write down the names of our enemies, if we have harmed them. It takes a lot of courage and honesty to really look at the bad relationships we have developed and see if we have been in the wrong. This is where working with someone else really helps. Many times we're too close to the situation to see it objectively. None of us like to admit fault when someone we don't like is involved, but we try to look at the relationship honestly, without letting our resentment blind us to the truth. Did we gossip about someone, spreading vicious lies or omitting part of the truth, damaging that person's reputation? Did we demonstrate our resentment by defiantly staring at them when they talked to us, or by being flippant and disrespectful? We put their names down, even if we just suspect we might have harmed them.

Many of us will have a problem adding some names to our lists, especially those of us who must include our perpetrator among those we have harmed. This is probably the last person we would ever dream of making amends to; it's too much like forgiving. But, if it's appropriate, we list them among those we have harmed as an act of faith necessary for our healing.

If we were abused by our parents, and at some time stole money or property from them, then we owe amends for that theft. We may even have used their sickness and dysfunction as a means of getting things we wanted. If a brother was the perpetrator and we harmed him, by lying about him or deliberately getting him in trouble with authorities, then we need to write down his name, too. And, if we want to forgive our abuser, that's fine, but we must give ourselves the time we need to prepare for something so important. Right now, we aren't even making amends—we are just writing down names.

We will never be *required* to forgive anyone; however, we may discover that our rage is really an unconscious attempt to protect ourselves from further harm by keeping other people at a distance. But, as we work these Steps, we will begin to see that we only hurt ourselves by holding on to that hurt and pain. As long as we continue to isolate ourselves from the warmth of human companionship, we will continue to suffer. Our abusers have never shared our pain! So, though we won't be asked to forgive anyone, we will try to become neutral toward them. And, perhaps later, we will *choose* to forgive them.

Some of us have a problem forgiving ourselves, especially if we enjoyed the caresses, the physical aspects of the abuse or the pseudo-love we received. We now accept that, for some of us, that was the only way we ever received nurturing or love.

Tammy shared: My parents never gave me love or even mild affection. When my teacher touched me and told me she loved me, I turned to her with open arms, starved for any kind of affection I could get.

We need to remember that we are physical, sexual beings. When we are touched in certain areas and in certain ways, our bodies become aroused and the touching feels good. This doesn't make the abuse good, and it doesn't make us bad. It just makes us human. We now understand where the responsibility lies, and accept that we were not at fault and that our bodies were only reacting in the way nature intended them to react.

Some of us have become so judgmental that we think we should be perfect, never making mistakes or doing wrong. As we work through these Steps, we begin to understand that we are not saints. And, once we acknowledge that we are looking for progress, not perfection, it gets easier to relax and stop beating up on ourselves. As we begin to accept ourselves for who and what we are, we are better able to forgive ourselves and to learn to love ourselves as human beings.

As with any of the Steps, if we encounter difficulties or what we face seems too painful, we ask our Higher Power to help us work through our problems. We ask that force beyond ourselves for the strength and willingness to get on with our lives.

The last part of this Step says, "and became willing to make amends to them all." After we make our list, we are to pause in our recovery to prepare ourselves to make amends to all those we have harmed. In this age of instant jello, instant coffee and instant mashed potatoes, we may want instant healing, but simply including a name on our list may not mean we are ready to even look that person in the eye, let alone make amends. We ask our Higher Power to help us become willing, to help us continue on our path of recovery.

For some of us, just working the Steps this far is enough motivation to make us willing to make amends to those we have harmed. For others, it will take more effort. We might be willing to make amends to some people, but not even willing to consider making amends to others. We talk with our Higher Power about this, and ask for help to become willing. We are the people who continue to be harmed by our defects and by our unwillingness to clean up our past mistakes. We ask for willingness, maybe just to be "willing to be willing." If that's all we can manage right now, that's okay.

As we continue through the Steps, and improve our relationships, we will become willing to make amends. When we realize that our unwillingness is preventing us from completing our recovery and fully experiencing serenity and peace, we are motivated to become willing. We once again give ourselves healing time in preparation for making amends. We stop rushing around doing things just for the sake of getting them over with, and call on our Higher Power to heal the deep wounds of incest and sexual abuse. We ask for the grace, confidence and readiness needed to participate in the amends process. By turning to our Higher Power, we don't have to make the amends on our own—we have a special friend on our side. We continue to ask our Higher Power for willingness and strength as we continue on our journey through the Steps and into recovery.

Step Eight Questions

▸ Are you using your Fourth-Step Inventory to make the list of all persons you have harmed?

▸ Are you putting everyone you have hurt on this list—even those you aren't yet ready to make amends with?

▸ Did you put your name at the top of the list?

▸ Are you willing to look honestly at the harm you have done to others?

▸ Are you remembering that, if you didn't harm them, they don't belong on the list?

▸ Do you believe that there is no one you have ever harmed?

▸ Do you believe that there are people you have harmed, but that "they deserved it"?

▸ If you didn't actually harm anyone, did you list them anyway because you're used to taking the blame for everything?

▸ Have you examined every relationship in your life to see what wrongs you might have done?

▸ Have you listed people, businesses and organizations that you have harmed?

▸ Have you listed everyone, including people who are dead or whose names you can't remember?

▸ Do you think that this list has to be perfect and complete in order to be "right"?

▸ Are you remembering that this list can be added to at any time?

▸ Are there some people whose names you can't remember, but who you know you harmed?

▸ Have you asked your Higher Power to help you make this list?

▸ Does the thought of making this list make you afraid or angry?

▸ Are you willing to put things right with yourself?

▸ Are you able to look at your self-destructive behaviors honestly?

▸ Are you willing to change?

▸ Are you willing to integrate your inner children into your life?

▸ Are you willing to be the person you truly are, not someone who meets everyone else's expectations?

▸ Are you willing to forgive yourself for your past mistakes?

▸ Are you willing to accept yourself?

▶ If you need someone else's input, are you seeking that help?

▶ Are you willing to accept responsibility for your actions?

▶ Can you stop punishing yourself for being abused?

▶ Are you beginning to focus on your own issues?

▶ Are you examining your motives for your actions?

▶ Are you worrying about how to make amends with the people you don't like?

▶ If you aren't willing to make certain amends, are you "willing to be willing"?

▶ Have you asked your Higher Power for the willingness to make amends where necessary?

▶ Is your unwillingness holding you back from full recovery?

▶ Are you afraid that making amends will be too difficult?

▶ Do you remember that this is a process, not an instantaneous happening?

▶ Are you being patient with yourself, giving yourself time to heal and to become willing?

Step Nine

We made direct amends to such people wherever possible, except when to do so would injure them or others.

Step Nine

In Step Eight, we made a list of all persons we had harmed and became willing to make amends to them all. Step Nine is the beginning of making those amends.

We turn to our dictionary again for a definition of the word *amends*. It says, *something given or done to make up for injury, loss, etc. that one has done*. This is different from an apology, which is a statement expressing regret for a fault or offense. The amends require a plan of action and an indication of a change. An apology is a means of stating our conscious awareness of an event or incident. It does not require a change or substitution of new behaviors, feelings and reactions to the same or similar situations. To make amends does not mean that we go to the people on our list saying we're sorry, over and over again. So many of us took on the role of apologist—no matter what happened, we were sorry about it and we apologized left and right, whether it was our fault or not. We now realize that every wrong is not our fault. If we did nothing to harm someone, then we don't have to apologize because something didn't go right, or someone had their feelings hurt. There will be times when the only thing we need to say will be "I'm sorry," but we can say it honestly and sincerely, not as an automatic response. Making amends means we are going to try to correct matters between others and ourselves. This won't always be possible, but we will do the best we can.

This Step doesn't mean that we're going to go to these people asking for forgiveness either. That isn't our purpose. Whether or not these people ever forgive us isn't the point. We just try our best to correct the past with each individual on our list.

We remember that our Higher Power is with us at all times, even through the most difficult situations. Because we've been strengthening our relationship with our Higher Power, we have the courage to do this Step. When we falter, we ask our Higher Power for the power and the willingness to keep going. Nothing is too difficult with our Higher Power's help.

We will learn more about courage and honesty as we go through this Step, and we will learn discipline, too. Discipline is training that develops self-control, personal empowerment and character. Many of us were "disciplined" as children, but, because it took the form of another sort of abuse, we haven't wanted anything to do with discipline. It has been too scary for us. But now we can begin to use self-discipline, we can nurture ourselves so that we can develop our self-control and rebuild our character. We will change from a person who reacts without thinking into someone who accepts their own feelings and consciously chooses how to act.

By making these amends, we will learn how to work through difficult situations instead of avoiding them, backing down from them, or becoming so upset about them that we can't function effectively. We will realize that we can discuss our mistakes with others and still be safe. We won't die. We won't be abused. We will do what we need to do, and then it will be over. We take care in choosing the people we trust so that we can continue to be safe. To the best of our ability, we will learn to recognize unsafe people and steer clear of them.

This Step will also help us learn how to confront others with their mistakes, and to stick up for our rights when necessary. Sometimes we've known we were right, but we let others walk all over us because we were afraid to take action for ourselves.

> **Kathy shared:** I never wanted anyone else to be upset, I wanted to keep peace at any cost, even if it meant I had to back down and discount myself. After I started making some of my amends, I realized that I could get through these scary things and still be okay. I found that I became more courageous in other types of situations, and I started to take a stand for my rights.

Some of us wondered whether it was all that important to make these amends. We rationalized that probably everyone knew we were sorry anyway, so why bother going through all the hassle of looking people up or making calls. And besides, what about the people whose names we've forgotten, or who have died?

Sharon, abused by her uncle when she was ten, asked her sponsor how hard she had to try to find someone on her list. She was told: "If that person owed you $10,000, how hard would you look for her? That's how much energy you need to invest in your search for the people on your list."

It's vital for our recovery that we make these amends. This is an important part of our clearing up the wreckage and garbage of the past. We can't assume that people know we regret our negative actions. We have to find them and tell them directly that we would like to make amends for our wrongs.

There will be some people on our list that we can't make amends to: they have died, we can't remember their names or their names have changed. For those who have died, there are several methods we can use to make amends. We can write a letter stating our feelings and what happened. Some of us may actually feel the need to mail the letter addressed to this person somewhere in heaven. Others have a mental conversation with the deceased, talking with them as if they truly could hear and understand. Still others talk with our Higher Power, letting that unseen force know our desire and willingness to make amends.

For those people that we can't find, we might write a letter to them and mail it, even though we don't know where they are living at present. The faith and trust we have in our Higher Power will somehow let the right person know how we feel. We can acknowledge to our Higher Power that we would like to make amends, and remain ready at all times to make those amends if we ever find those people.

Melissa shared that she owed amends to a woman she had worked with fifteen years earlier, but she couldn't remember her last name. Two years after she made her amends list, Melissa did remember that woman's last name, and immediately looked her up in the phone book: "I couldn't find her name listed, but now I have that woman's last name written down so that I can check in other cities when I travel."

When it is physically impossible to make direct amends in situations like these, we might make indirect amends by doing something good for someone else while thinking about the person to whom we owe amends. We can give of our time, talents and energy for the sake of the person to whom we wish to make amends. Or we could make a donation to a charity in that person's name.

> **Henry shared what happened to him when he realized he had multiple personalities:** I was sure that I owed many people amends for things I had done when one of my alters was out, but because I don't remember everything, it's impossible to make amends for all the harm I've done. I have done the best I can, making amends for the things I can remember, and I just hope that some day I

will be able to remember everything and be willing to complete my amends.

When we wrote our amends list, most of us put our own names at the top, for we were the ones most harmed by our actions. Although we have already begun to make amends, we still tend to be our own worst critics. But, in order to be healthy, we need to release our self-directed anger and negativity. Once we do this, we begin to like—or even *love*—ourselves again, confident that we did the best we could with the knowledge and skills that we had at that time. As we look at our past conduct, we realize that, though our coping skills weren't the best, they did help us to survive—especially through the abuse. Having acknowledged this, we are free to forgive ourselves once and for all.

> **Mary Beth told her sponsor that for years she would bemoan her past mistakes:** I'd look back and say, "if only I had said this," or "if only I had done that." Through working these Steps, I now realize that I couldn't have done things any differently. I didn't know any better then. If I were to do the same negative things now, that would be wrong, but back then I was getting by the best I could. I have learned to stop punishing myself for all the *if only's* in my life. I am learning to live in the present by correcting my past the best I can and making plans for my future as I overcome my destructive behavior.

Looking at our list, we consider just one individual with whom to begin. We make a plan of how, when and where we propose to make the amends. When we consider just *one* person, the task is not so overwhelming that we decide it's all too much and never make amends at all.

There are many places where we can approach this person—a quiet lunch, a meeting at work, a walk in the park, a family reunion—whatever the setting, our Higher Power will help us feel safe with our new direction and growth. We accept the risk and begin.

Next on most of our amends lists will be those we think will be most receptive—probably our spouses or significant others, and our immediate families. Because we've spent a lot of time with these people, they probably have borne the brunt of our character defects. We tell them face-to-face that we realize that some of our past actions have hurt them, and we're sorry. We let them know that we love them and that we are in the process of changing our lives. We tell them we'd like to correct the situation if we can, and that we'll act differently in the future when similar situations occur.

Now, we move on to slightly more difficult amends, perhaps those with friends or co-workers. Again, we talk with them in person where possible, and let them know we're in the process of changing our lives around, and that we need to make amends for our wrongs. There usually isn't a need to be specific about what we've done, whether to family, friends, acquaintances or institutions. They know the details all too well. If the list of specific incidents is long, we simply indicate that we know now that our behavior was unacceptable and that we'd like to do better in the future. We tell them we're sorry, if that's appropriate, and we make a polite exit.

We are making amends for our errors, so we keep our statements in the "I ..." form as we humbly make our amends. We are not trying to justify our actions or to assert our opinions or our rights; we are making a sincere attempt to correct our previous actions and reactions. We are making an honest change of direction on our path to recovery.

Sometimes the other person simply isn't willing to give up what they consider justifiable anger toward us. In such a case, we let the person know we regret our actions, and that if it were possible we would change how we acted. Then we leave, knowing that we've done our part, we've taken the action necessary for our recovery.

Some people will calmly accept what we're saying and doing; some will blow it off with a "no big deal." There will be others who will say, "Oh, you don't need to do this," or, "But I don't remember anything happening." There is no need to get involved in a big discussion. We might tell them that we do need to do this, not so much for their sake as for our own recovery.

And then there will be the people who don't accept our amends at all, who will be belligerent or resentful. Some will want to dredge up the old wrongs again and argue with us. We allow them to say whatever they need to say, but don't argue or join in the debate. We also guard against blaming them or pointing out their faults. That isn't our purpose. We thank them for sharing, thank them for their time, and leave. To persist, or to try to change their views, will only keep the wounds open, when what we are doing is healing our past. We aren't responsible for the other person's actions or reactions, we are only responsible for our own. When we go to someone in a sincere attempt to make amends, and they refuse to accept them, that is the other person's responsibility, not ours. We have done our part, and that is all we can do. We remember that we are doing this for our recovery, not to please anyone else or to get anyone to forgive us. When we are very clear about our actions and our motives, life is easier and we can make these amends simply and thoroughly.

Perhaps the most difficult amends to make will be to those people that we still don't like, that we have no intention of ever becoming friendly with, and with whom we don't want any further relationship. It's very hard to go to someone we can't tolerate and acknowledge our wrongs. This takes a tremendous amount of courage and discipline, but we go through with it because we know to stop is to not recover. And we want to recover.

This is not to say that we owe amends to the perpetrators in our lives for any aspect of the abuse we suffered. We were not responsible for the abuse, they were. If we haven't harmed them in some other manner, then we don't owe them any amends. Thinking evil thoughts about them, hating them, planning their destruction in our minds, these might not be good for us any longer, but they didn't hurt the abusers. Contrary to what a lot of us believe, other people cannot read our minds. We don't owe anyone amends for what we think or feel. Only if we have acted on those thoughts and done something harmful do we owe amends.

If we've taken or damaged others' property, we will have to make some type of restitution. To repay a store for stolen property, it may be possible to pay the injured party directly, or send money with an anonymous note explaining what we did. When direct amends are not possible, a charitable contribution in the name of the injured party is a good option. To make restitution to a current employer for stolen supplies or time, a few extra hours worked without pay may be in order.

For every instance of wrongdoing on our part, we offer the best and most suitable amends. This might even include being willing to go to jail to pay for our mistakes. If we have committed crimes, then we must be willing to pay the price for them and for our recovery.

We have to be very careful here, however. We look at the part of this Step that says, "except when to do so would injure them or others." If others will be harmed by our inability to work because we're in jail, for instance if our family will be destitute, then we don't carry it that far. We must be willing, however, to do even that if the circumstances warrant. These situations should be discussed thoroughly with someone else, perhaps a sponsor or a therapist, before we take action. Yes, we want to clear up our past, but not at the expense of others' well-being.

Other situations in which we wouldn't make direct amends would be when to do so would injure the other person. For instance, if our significant other has no idea that we've been unfaithful, we don't go to them and tell them about it. This would hurt them far more than their not knowing ever did. We don't buy our recovery at other people's expense. It would be better to rededicate ourselves to our significant other and become a more loving and caring person in the relationship.

It would also do more harm than good to make direct amends when we have gossiped about someone. We should not approach someone and say, "I'm sorry I gossiped about you," when they had no idea anything had ever been said. However, if their reputation has suffered because of the gossip, we do admit our mistakes and make whatever corrections are possible. One possibility is to go to the persons with whom we gossiped and let them know we were wrong and that we won't be doing that anymore.

If someone was harmed by our not taking responsibility for some wrong, we must be willing to correct that situation publicly.

> **Paul told us:** I had let a guy at work take the blame for a mistake that I had made. He was overlooked for a promotion as a result of my action. I had to go to our boss and explain to her what I had done, and I let everyone at work know that I had made the mistake, not the other guy. It was painful, but now I'm glad I did it.

There will be people on our list that we can't go to in person to make amends. A phone call or letter will suffice. Just because we can't make our amends face-to-face shouldn't stop us. The phone call or the letter doesn't have to go into details or take a lot of time. We briefly explain what we are doing and why, and say that we regret our past actions, just as we do with the in-person amends we make.

With everybody on our list, including ourselves, we make what are called *living amends*. This is another way of saying that we're going to do things differently from now on.

For several years, Jessie was forced to participate in ritualistic abuse and felt that she had never had control over her own body. She began making living amends to herself by visiting her doctor regularly and getting her blood pressure under control. She began walking daily, not only for her physical well-being, but also for her mental well-being. "I found that when I took my life back and claimed myself as my own, I could see how my reactions or inactions had hurt those I loved the most. I was able to talk to those people about the wrongs I had done to them, and begin making positive changes."

Many people do something hurtful, say they're sorry, then a week later repeat the same mistake; and they do this over and over. If this is our pattern, we need to change it. As the old saying goes, "actions speak louder than words." When we make a mistake the first time, it's appropriate to apologize. Then we examine our thinking and actions to see what we can change so the sequence of events is different the next time. And we gradually begin making those behavioral changes.

> **Jean shared this story:** I spent a lot of time avoiding reality by reading books. My children would come up to me asking me to pay attention to them somehow, and I would brush them off. Now when they approach me, or even sometimes before they do, I put my book down and give them my time and attention.

Perhaps we've been arrogant or demanding with sales people. To make amends to those we've harmed as a group, we consciously treat the next sales clerk or waitress with respect and courtesy. If we've been crazy drivers, cutting people off or blasting our horns, we change our behavior and let people change lanes in peace. Our living amends with ourselves are to change our self-destructive behavior, whether it's as extreme as cutting ourselves or as ordinary as not getting enough sleep.

As we go through our list, we cross off the names of those to whom we've made amends. Even as we are working through our list, we may remember some people we need to add. Until all the names are crossed off, we keep the list available so that we are reminded to make the necessary amends as opportunities occur.

When we've made our amends, or as many as we possibly can, we realize that we've come a long way in our recovery. It's a great feeling to know that we can now face anyone, anytime, anywhere, look them in the eye and know, deep down, that our part of the relationship is healed. We lay down the burden of guilt and shame we've been carrying all these years, and rejoice in our lightness.

Once we have begun on this Step, and are going through our amends list to the best of our ability, we will realize that we are able to do things that we never dreamed possible before, because we are trusting in our Higher Power. We will be able to look at our past calmly, without panic, fear, guilt or shame. We will start to accept our responsibilities and we will acknowledge what are other people's responsibilities. We will start to set boundaries for ourselves so that we are safe, and so that we don't spill over into other people's lives. We will enter a state of serenity and peace. Our attitudes toward ourselves and others will change. We will begin to accept ourselves as being the best people we know how to be today, and that others are doing their best, too. Their actions may not meet our expectations, but we will finally accept that they don't have to. This acceptance will become our way of life. As we continue working these Steps and trusting in our Higher Power, many of our fears will disappear, and we'll see a new hope for our future.

Step Nine Questions

▸ Before you start the amends, are you asking your Higher Power for the courage and strength to do them?

▸ Are you inviting that force beyond yourself to guide you while you make amends?

▶ If the first person on your list is yourself, have you begun making amends?

▶ Have you begun changing the way you think about yourself?

▶ Are you beginning to change your self-talk?

▶ Are you beginning to accept that you did the best you could to survive?

▶ Do you have reasonable expectations and goals for yourself?

▶ Are you keeping your life as easy and simple as possible?

▶ Are you taking better care of yourself?

▶ Are you establishing boundaries for yourself?

▶ Are you standing up for your rights when necessary?

▶ Are you making living amends by changing negative behavior?

▶ Are you making your amends with others with no expectations that they will change?

▶ Have you thought of different ways to make amends that will work for you?

▶ Are you making direct, personal amends where possible?

▶ Have you made phone calls or written letters and mailed them?

▶ Are you making an honest effort to find the people on your list, or just going through the motions?

▶ Are you using the amends as an excuse to justify your actions?

▶ Are you using the amends to hurt someone who has hurt you?

▶ As you make the amends, are you crossing the names off your list?

► If you think of others that you have harmed, are you adding them to the list?

► Are you keeping your amends simple in explanation and details?

► Are you honestly trying to put things right between you and others?

► If the other person tries to start the fight all over again, are you able to distance yourself and not get involved?

► Are you expecting forgiveness from others?

► Are you expecting others to apologize for what they did?

► Before you make amends, are you examining the situation from all angles in an attempt to avoid new hurts?

► Before you make amends, are you planning the best way to do so, not just leaping in with no thought?

► If no one else would be injured, are you willing to go to any lengths to make the amends?

► Have you looked at various methods of making restoration?

► Are you using this Step to clean up the past?

► Are you using this Step to strengthen your life?

► Can you believe that this will be the beginning of a new start in life, with a clean slate?

► Can you believe that you no longer have to carry around that excess baggage unless you want to?

► Are you apologizing to people, but not making any changes?

► Are you still apologizing when you haven't done anything wrong?

► If it is impossible to make direct amends, are you seeking ways to make amends indirectly?

NOTES

Step Ten

We continued to take personal inventory, and when we were wrong promptly admitted it.

Step Ten

The Steps we have worked so far, as completely as possible at this time, have been those necessary to clean up our share of the past. The first two Steps are the admission of our problem and the solution to that problem. Step Three begins our journey into change when we make that decision to trust our Higher Power with our thinking and our actions. Steps Four through Nine are the actions necessary for us to discover our errors and correct them.

Through working and living these Steps, we have discovered a new person within ourselves. We have used the Steps as tools to look at ourselves and as stepping stones to a better life.

The remaining three Steps are to be done on a daily basis, for the rest of our lives. Some people call them the *maintenance* Steps, others call them the *living* Steps. They help us continue the growth we started at the beginning, when we admitted our powerlessness over sexual abuse. Rather than maintaining our changes, they help us to continue to change and to grow, spiritually and emotionally, and to live the rest of our lives in the best way we can. When we were still living in resentment and fear, we weren't able to enjoy life fully or to reach our full potential. These Steps will enable us to achieve far more than we ever thought possible, and they will help us to stay in fit spiritual condition.

Step Ten tells us to continue to take inventory of our actions, and when we make mistakes to correct them immediately. It combines Steps Three through Nine, to be done on a daily basis. The first inventory that we did for Step Four helped us clean up our past. Step Five through Step Nine helped us come to terms with ourselves and that past. Most of us experienced a great sense of peace when we finished these Steps. Step Ten will help us to nurture and deepen that sense of peace and serenity.

Step Ten helps us affirm our progress and continue to look closely at ourselves so no new character defects or shortcomings appear to consume and control our lives, or to interfere with our restoration as functioning human beings. It keeps us from slipping backward or merely changing our methods of dysfunction and unmanageability; we don't want to jump from drinking to spending to gambling, deluding ourselves into believing we're recovering.

As with the other Steps, we ask for help from a force beyond ourselves in doing our daily inventory. We ask for the strength to do it every day, and we ask for help to be honest and sincere in our efforts. This Tenth-Step Inventory will be a daily look at our lives. It will be a personal inventory, helping us to recognize many of the same character defects we have been working on from the start. As we continue to see them, we will take action to change our behavior, and make amends when necessary.

Our recovery will be a lifetime process, because growth is a lifetime process. Sometimes along the way, we may get tired and think, "I can't do this anymore. Enough already!" That's okay. We can take a very short rest every once in a while. However, if we try to rest too long, we'll start sliding back into the old habits and thinking, and eventually we could end up right back where we started.

Cheryl, who had been abused by her mother when she was young, found this to be true the hard way. She was a recovering alcoholic who had been working on her abuse issues for 2 years: I felt that I had done enough. I had cleaned up my past; I had even forgiven my mother. I'd worked and looked at my life and felt that I had moved beyond all that and could stop working. I was alright for about six months, then I started getting angry at people, I started treating them—and myself—like I did before working the Steps. Pretty soon I started taking a drink or two to help me get through the day. Luckily, an old friend who knew what I'd gone through confronted me with the truth, and I went back to meetings and started with the Steps again. I hope I never get that cocky again.

During our continuing inventories, we watch for resentments, selfishness, dishonesty and fear. These four defects seem to affect almost every aspect of our lives, because they hold us back from living fully. Sometimes we can think of these four as the major headings of shortcomings, with everything else grouped under them.

Resentment is usually our number one problem. We hate it when other people seem to be picking on us, or are mean to us. We resent our boss for criticizing our work, even though it might need that correction. We get angry at the other driver who isn't going as fast as we want him to go. We resent our children for taking so much time and energy when all we want to do is just sit and watch the soap operas, or relax in peace and quiet. Our spouse or significant other doesn't leap into action to do whatever we want, so we're angry.

We can find all kinds of reasons to be resentful every day. Sometimes it's even justified; other people *are* sometimes wrong or hurtful. We ask ourselves in these situations whether our actions were at fault in any way, and, if so, we take steps to change and make whatever amends are necessary. There will be times when we are not at fault. Then we let go of the resentment, perhaps not taking any action at all, or perhaps taking care of our needs by asking for clarification, restitution or whatever is necessary.

We have become very defensive in our roles as survivors of abuse. It may be difficult to distinguish between legitimate and unacceptable requests from others, and it can be difficult to spot our own faults, overreactions or misinterpretations. Many of us have become champion excuse-givers. We can find anything or anyone else to blame for our problems or difficulties. It is often easier to blame others when things go wrong or we become uncomfortable in a situation. If the source of a problem is "out there," then we don't have to look inside ourselves and accept responsibility for our wrongs. As we become aware of this defensive attitude, we start to change it and take responsibility when it is properly ours to take.

Fear can be devastating for us. We fall into fear so easily, perhaps because we lived in fear for so long that it seems natural for us. Sometimes it feels like almost any situation can trigger our fear, and we become that abused victim again. Through the Steps we start to outgrow fear. In our daily inventory, we become aware of our *fear triggers,* what situations or people cause us to become fearful. We can then start to look at the reality of the situation. We can ask ourselves how rational it is to be afraid of each situation. We can analyze what has happened, and we can seek out someone else's help if we need help in getting to the core issues surrounding our fears.

Many times we're unable to convince ourselves or our inside kids that we're safe, but when we hear it from someone else, then we can believe it. We can begin to grow, to take risks. People who live in fear don't take risks, they want everything to stay the same so they can be safe. Unfortunately for those of us with that attitude, life is change, and we need to learn how to cope with it in a safe, rational manner. These Steps help us to learn to do that safely, a little at a time.

Dishonesty is often a problem for sexual abuse survivors. Many of us learned to lie, distort the truth, or not tell the whole truth, to keep ourselves safe. Now that we're learning a program of honesty, we look at these old habits and start to change them. We are beginning to learn trust, in ourselves, our Higher Power and others, so we don't have to lie or cheat to be safe. We find that we can't continue to deceive others, or ourselves, any longer. We have to start trusting others, and they have to be able to trust us. Each day we need to be aware of when we've twisted things around, just a little bit, and if we've harmed someone else by doing that, then we make amends to them and to anyone else who might be involved.

> **Bonnie learned early in life that if she made herself look more capable or more important than the people around her that her mother wouldn't abuse her so much. She started adding a little bit extra to a story, or she'd tell the truth, but change her voice inflections and her facial expressions to indicate that she didn't really mean what she was saying:** When I started doing a Tenth Step every day, I realized exactly how often I was doing things like that, and I saw how it hurt others, either their feelings—if they were present—or their reputations. I can't do that anymore. I want others to be able to trust me, and to trust that what I say is the truth. Sometimes now when I start doing that, I hear myself, and I change what I'm saying to reflect the true situation. I feel so much better about myself when I'm able to do that.

Selfishness can be a real issue for survivors of abuse. We learned early that we had to snatch what we could when we could, or we most likely would not get anything—whether it was attention, love, food, or something else. For many of us, being the class clown or always trying to be the focus of attention in some other way helped us feel validated, to feel that we existed and had some purpose for being alive. They also served as a defense, to keep people at a distance—while we were "on stage" we couldn't be expected to interact with people one-on-one, and no one could guess the truth about our pain and hurt. To share something could be traumatic and could feel like we were giving up a part of ourselves.

> **Jennie was abused by her father and older brother when she was young. She became a compulsive eater, learning that when she ate, she didn't feel the pain as much:** I would watch people at dinner or at parties, sharing their desserts, or discovering a new taste and giving to others so they could experience it, too. That was utterly foreign to me. I couldn't do that if my life depended on it. I still have trouble sharing food. It takes a real effort on my part to offer some of my food to others, even my children. It feels wrenching, actually physically painful. But I do it now, because it gets less painful the further into recovery I get, and it's a real lesson for me to consider others; their wants and needs. For me to even think of sharing is a big step, and when I'm actually able to give something away, it's hard, but it feels good, too.

Other survivors have gone to the other extreme, always giving anything and everything to others—our time, our energy, our selves—in an effort to feel wanted and loved. Those of us who can't say no to anyone haven't learned where our boundaries are: where we stop and other people begin. We became so enmeshed with our perpetrators or our dysfunctional families and friends that we never learned to separate, to be distinct people on our own. These deeply ingrained character traits can be very difficult to change. But change is possible with daily effort and awareness. It can be hard work. It can be interesting work. And it most definitely *will* be rewarding work.

In continuing to take personal inventory, we will use several different types: a spot check, a daily inventory, a weekly inventory, and an annual formal inventory. Each type serves a valuable purpose in our recovery. This might sound like a lot of work, but once we start doing these things, they become automatic and are, in fact, important tools in our growth.

These inventories will keep us grounded in reality, and in touch with our lives as they are unfolding today. Tenth-Step Inventories prevent us from putting our walls of denial back up, and slipping back into old patterns of behavior. Some of us even keep a written copy of our inventories so we will have a record of our progress. By trying different ways of taking these inventories, and finding the one(s) we are most comfortable with in our new lives, we will continue to improve ourselves on an ongoing basis.

The *spot check inventory* is one we use throughout the day. We become aware of our thinking and our actions on an hourly, sometimes even minute-by-minute, basis. We do this all day, every day. When we realize that we're angry, or fearful, or acting selfishly, we pause in our actions and take a look at what's happening. Many times, especially when we've just begun our recovery process, we find ourselves reacting in the same old negative ways. Now, however, because we are aware of our faults and are watching for them, we can see when we are falling into the old habits and we can change our behavior.

Maybe at first we won't recognize our defects until a couple of days after-the-fact. For instance, perhaps one of our shortcomings is the use of sarcasm, which can be very hurtful to others. Gradually, through the process of working Step Ten daily, we start to recognize when we are being sarcastic and hurtful sooner. Pretty soon, only a few hours go by before we realize that it happened again. Then, with continued practice, we become aware of it while we are actually doing it. At that point, we can stop, let the other person know that we slipped into old behavior, and start again. Finally, over time, we stop using sarcasm at all—it just doesn't occur to us and we don't like to hear it anymore, from ourselves or others. As we work toward recovery, we will be able to utilize these new tools to correct our old habits and make amends when we fall into our old ways.

At night, before we are too tired to think straight, we do our *daily inventory*. We look back through the day just past, searching for anger or resentments, fear, selfishness, or dishonesty. If our character defects influenced our actions during the day, we examine the situation. We try to figure out where we went wrong, or what was the trigger for us, so that in the future we can change how we react in similar situations. If we said or did something that hurt or injured someone in our daily interactions, we talk to them as soon as possible and correct the situation. We might need to talk with a sponsor or some other impartial observer to help us determine whether we were at fault.

In our nightly inventory, we also look for the good things we have done throughout the day. This is a great time to find the positives—the times we acted differently than we ever have before. We look for changes and improvements in our behavior. Even if it doesn't feel like much of a change. Even if it's just a tiny little change. We celebrate that, and we thank our Higher Power for the help we've been given to make those changes. We look at the new behaviors we used during the day that we would like to make a permanent part of the the new person we are slowly becoming. We think of ways to continue to make that new process an integral part of our thinking and actions each day. We ask our Higher Power to help us to see ourselves as we really are, and to help us with the problems we can't presently handle.

This nightly inventory is an opportunity to take a continuous look at our liabilities and our assets. So many of us have felt that we're total goof-offs, that we never do anything right, that we are total failures. This is the time to recognize and acknowledge that we are good people and we do good things. Perhaps we'd like to call someone to help us celebrate our improvements. It helps to get validation from others in our successes, even the teeny ones.

We can write down this nightly inventory if that helps us see things more clearly. Other things that we might want to write down in addition to our defects and our assets would be anything that came up during the day that we forgot to deal with in our Fourth-Step Inventory. Perhaps we remember something we had blocked out before, or we see something from a different perspective. We take this opportunity to investigate those memories and those emotions. We may need to discuss them with someone else. Perhaps what we remember might be so overwhelming that we can't deal with it right away. We need to take as long as we need to deal with it, or to work it through with our sponsor.

After going through this Tenth-Step process for awhile, we will get better at seeing things clearly and honestly. We won't always need to check with others for clarification. There will be days when we find nothing negative; these are the days we can truly celebrate.

> **Bob, who was abused by his older brother, told us about the first time he couldn't find any defects in his day:** I was astounded. I thought, "This can't be right. I must have forgotten something, or misinterpreted something." I thought I must have done something wrong. What an incredible feeling to realize that I'd actually had a whole day that was positive and upbeat. It truly was my first miracle. I marked that date with a big star and am using it as an example of hope for many more miraculous days.

A *weekly inventory* is a review of our activities for the most recent week. We think about it, asking ourselves if it was a growth week, or just another week that we have passed through. Did we do something good for ourselves during the week? Did we find ourselves mood-altering by falling back into old patterns and responses? Did we fall into our old addictions, again? If so, then we acknowledge this slip, make amends to ourselves and/or to others, and start again on our pathway toward recovery. We are continually striving for progress, not perfection. We always remember to be kind and gentle with ourselves. We've been abused too often; we don't need to beat ourselves up for our mistakes.

Occasionally, perhaps every 6 months to a year, we will write down an inventory similar to the one we did in Step Four. Some people use the end of the calendar year as a review time to mark their progress. Others use the anniversary of the day that they personally made the decision to change their ineffective behavior patterns to review how far they have come and how much farther they have to go. This helps us to stay on track, and keeps us from skipping over missed issues.

All of these inventories require an honest look at our actions and our thinking. Then we can ask our Higher Power to help us remove our shortcomings, just as we did originally in Step Six and Step Seven. We make amends when needed. Although we don't owe amends to anyone for our thoughts, we want to be aware of our negative thinking, because negative thoughts may cause us to act inappropriately and end up needing to make amends to someone.

While some people may think it's acceptable to apologize and do the same thing two days later, apologizing is not making amends. Amends require an honest effort to change our behavior. Continuing the same behavior and thinking everything will be okay just because we said we're sorry is not what we're aiming for. We're working toward change.

Everything we do in this program is for our personal benefit. In the long run, it will benefit those around us, but basically we do this work to help ourselves. To try to smooth over a situation without making any changes inside ourselves doesn't work. At first, when we start to make these changes, we will make mistakes and repeat negative behavior, but we watch for our old habits, and correct them ever sooner in the process, until we have completely replaced them with new, positive behaviors.

When looking at our day, or a situation, or the last several months, we concentrate on looking for our part in whatever happened. We look to see what part belongs to us, and what part belongs to the others involved. When we have done wrong, we take care of it, we try to clean up our part. We need to be willing to admit our errors, so we can learn from them and continue to grow. If we have harmed someone, we must make amends quickly. We can't let these situations drag out, or pretty soon we'll be slipping back into old resentments and even building up new resentments. When we let negativity fester, we become negative in every aspect of our lives. If we've done wrong, we need to admit it and correct it where possible.

When the other person or persons are at fault, we remember that it isn't up to us to change them. If they have hurt us or done harm to us, we have to decide what action, if any, is appropriate for us to take. There will be times when there is absolutely nothing we can do to change the situation or the person. When that happens, we ask our Higher Power for the strength to go on without resentment or anger. Because there is nothing we can do about the situation, we acknowledge our feelings, probably talk about it with someone we trust, and we ask for help in moving beyond the hurt or the anger.

Sometimes it helps us to move on if we remember that other people have their own problems and concerns. There are some very sick people in this world, as we all know. Hurting people hurt other people. Just because we are healing does not mean that they are healing, too. Just because we are cleaning up our lives, and living in peace and serenity, and working hard to recover, does not mean that we won't have problems or that no one will ever hurt us again. Unfortunately, things like that will happen. The big difference is that now we have the tools and coping skills to help us get through the pain and anger. We don't have to take the negativity in and bear the other person's burden.

We are starting to realize where we end and where other people begin. We can forgive them if we want to. Or we don't have to forgive anyone. What we can't afford to do is to live in the resentment, the fear and the anger. If we can get rid of the resentment without forgiving people who hurt us, that's fine. If we do forgive those sick people, that's fine, too. We have learned to separate the individual from the dysfunctional behavior. We have come to understand the difference between a person who is just out to hurt others and someone who is hurting, but trying their best to recover. Because we are continuing our program of recovery every day, we can't predict what we will do or feel in 6 months, a year, 5 years.

> **Sally said:** One thing I learned through doing these Steps is to "never say never." I remember when I first started that I was vehement about never forgiving my father for abusing me. Now, after working hard for the last few years, I realize that he was the victim of his abuse and that I can't carry the burden of anger toward him any longer. I don't love him, and I don't have any contact with him, but I don't hate him anymore either.

When others are at fault, there may be times when we have to take action to protect ourselves or to take care of our needs. We are no longer willing to let anyone abuse us, in any situation. If someone at work lies about us, we talk with the people involved and tell them the truth. If a friend continually abuses our friendship, we tell them how we feel and what needs to be changed if the relationship is to continue. We aren't anyone's doormat any longer. We have rights, and we will stand fast when necessary.

We need to remember that we only hurt ourselves with our anger or resentment. The target of our anger is probably blithely going on his/her way, not even aware that we're seething with anger or losing sleep because of what they did to us. We are the ones not living in peace and serenity. We are the ones overeating, drugging, drinking, gambling, etc. They don't care about the effects of their actions on our lives. We have to be the ones who care, the ones who take steps to be peaceful and healed. It is a waste of our time and our energy to carry around resentment or fear because of other people. It can be very difficult to see this and to get to a point where we believe this to be true. We might have to start small, getting rid of tiny resentments, and work our way up to the big ones.

Something else we watch for are unreasonable expectations and demands. Many times we expect other people to act the way we want them to, and when they don't, we're hurt or angry. We have no right to expect anyone to act in a certain way, or even in a healthy way. When we place demands on others, we are not allowing them to be themselves. We're telling them who to be and how to act. That doesn't work. Just as we are learning to accept responsibility for our own actions, we must allow others to be responsible for their actions.

Many of us justify our interference by saying, "I was just trying to save her from making the same mistake I did." But maybe that person needs to make that same mistake so that she/he can learn and grow. And maybe it won't be a mistake for another person. We can't make judgments about right and wrong for other people. We let them make their own mistakes. We can't expect them to live to please us. We cannot place our goals, ideals and expectations on others just because we love them.

Another aspect of looking at our daily lives involves knowing when to stay with an opinion or a feeling that is right for us, but may not be right for others. Many of us don't trust our own judgments or feelings. If we express an opinion and someone says we're wrong, we tend to give way and allow that other person to rule us. When we have an opinion, or take an action that doesn't please someone else, we owe it to ourselves to stick by that opinion as long as we continue to believe it is valid—and to let it go *only* if we become convinced we are wrong. We start listening to our instincts and trusting them to be right for us. If it feels like we've done the right thing, and we haven't harmed anyone, then we don't apologize for it to anyone. We need to stand firm when people try to talk us into something that we know is not right. We are the only ones who know what is right for us, and we honor that and act on it.

How we continue on our personal path of recovery is each person's decision. Continuing to take personal inventory is a vital step in changing from a victim into a survivor and finally into a recovered human being. Changing old behaviors and old attitudes takes time, and can sometimes be difficult and painful. Throughout these inventories, we continue to look for the positive elements as well as the negative ones. We examine our errors, visualize ourselves doing better, and work toward change. Doing these inventories will require us to learn patience and persistence. We are patient with ourselves and realize that we won't change overnight. We will continue to make mistakes, right up until the day we die. But as long as we're persistent, and keep working toward improving our lives, then we reap the benefits of long term peace and serenity.

Step Ten Questions

‣ Are you doing an inventory daily, weekly, monthly, annually?

‣ Are you becoming more aware of your actions?

‣ Do you review your actions honestly?

‣ As you do your daily inventory, do you look for your positive as well as your negative actions?

‣ Are you watching out for denial and self-delusion as you do your inventory?

‣ Are you asking yourself each day, "When was I selfish, dishonest, resentful or afraid?"

▸ When you do something differently, do you congratulate yourself?

▸ When you slip into old habits, do you notice it and change them?

▸ Are you giving others the freedom to live their own lives and make their own mistakes?

▸ Do you still allow others to make your decisions, to tell you what to think or do?

▸ If someone says or does something hurtful, do you become obsessed about it, or do you examine the situation to see what part in it you played?

▸ If you were at fault, do you attempt to make amends?

▸ If you had no responsibility in the situation, are you able to feel the feelings and then get on with your life?

▸ Are you asking your Higher Power to help you to be honest with yourself and willing to change?

▸ Are you slowing down enough to listen for your Higher Power's will for you?

▸ During the day, do you spot check your behavior?

▸ Has it been a long time since your last Fourth-Step Inventory?

▸ Are the resentments and hurts starting to pile up again?

▸ Did you have a sense of peace when you started these Steps that you have since lost?

▸ Are you talking with someone safe to get reality checks when you need them?

▸ Are you open to taking risks that you wouldn't have considered before?

▸ As your old shortcomings disappear, are you replacing them with new compulsions or with healthy behavior?

► Are you giving yourself enough time to be thorough and honest?

► Have you inserted the "I" back into your life?

► When necessary, are you standing up for your rights?

► Are you expressing your feelings in a non-threatening manner?

► Are you setting appropriate boundaries?

► If someone crosses those boundaries, are you able to let them know?

► Are you beginning to feel more safe and less fearful?

► Are you starting to trust others more?

► Can other people trust you?

► Are you beginning to feel a sense of worth and value just because you are who you are?

► Are you beginning to say no to other people's demands, if that's appropriate?

► Are you able to separate yourself from others instead of being enmeshed in their lives?

► Are you thanking your Higher Power for the strength and courage you are receiving?

► Are you celebrating your victories?

Step Eleven

*We sought through prayer and meditation to improve
our conscious contact with our Higher Power
as we understood that Power, praying only for
knowledge of our Higher Power's will for us and the
power to carry that out.*

Step Eleven

All through this book we have referred to the spiritual part of the program; we have emphasized over and over again that we need the help and strength of our Higher Power to change and to grow. This Step is the action step we will be taking every day to seek that help, so we can continue the healing we have begun in the earlier Steps. We've been working on a new relationship with our Higher Power and this Step continues building that relationship into the most powerful tool we have for our recovery.

We will use prayer and meditation every day to seek our Higher Power's guidance. As survivors of sexual abuse, we often don't know what is good for us, and what might be harmful. Many of us were raised in dysfunctional families and we were never taught how to cope with life or how to make decisions. We developed our coping skills as best we could, and we're discovering that many of those skills are now harmful to us. Now we are learning to be more gentle and kind with ourselves. We *deserve* to have that universal force's strength and power in our lives, and we *need* to have knowledge of its will for us so that we can enhance our lives.

We rejoice in knowing that we are special people—strong, capable people. We have survived the abuse, and now, with our improving conscious contact with our Higher Power, we will conquer it.

There is no shame in relying on a force beyond ourselves. Perhaps an abuser tried to convince us we were weak people, especially if we prayed for help. But, as with all the lies we were told, this is not true. Throughout history people have depended on prayer to help them get through the bad times. Prayer and meditation are not just for the pious. Meditation and prayer will help anyone who wants and needs help from a force beyond themselves.

We don't apologize for using prayer or for relying on our Higher Power. After all, many of us developed some type of crutch to help us through: alcohol, compulsive eating, co-dependence, gambling. What better crutch could there be than to lean on the strength of our Higher Power. We are only human; we have had a very hard time surviving on our unaided strength alone.

Prayer and meditation are quite often interwoven; they can be done alone or together. Prayer, especially, can be used throughout the day to help us get through difficult situations. Prayer can be very formal. It can be any prayer from any religion that means something to us more than just words that we mouth because we happen to know them. Prayer can be as casual as "Please (addressed to any force beyond ourselves), I need your help now!" When we pray, we are talking with our Higher Power. We can actually carry on a conversation with that force, if that helps us.

> **Winnie found, by using prayer to talk with her Higher Power, her problems and concerns were not as great as they had seemed. Just being able to tell someone who would not judge or criticize helped her. She used some of her prayer time as a way of releasing her anger. She said:**
> I found that my God did not condemn me for my human

feelings. But the best thing for me about talking with God is that God never repeated a secret, like my mother and sisters did.

Just as prayer is talking to a Higher Power, meditation is listening. When we listen quietly and carefully, we often get answers to questions that used to bother us.

As with prayer, there are different ways to meditate. We can spend a lot of time in meditation, or we can take 5 minutes. We can't do this when we are busy doing and running; we need quiet time to just *be*. We get quiet and allow our Higher Power the chance to let us know what the plans for us are. We can meditate very formally, or we can be peaceful and simply let our minds wander where they will.

> **Molly told us:** I used to think meditation meant sitting in uncomfortable positions, saying "UUUUMMMMM," and contemplating my navel. I tried, but it just didn't work. Fortunately, since then I have found a method that works for me, and I get a lot of peace and many insights when I meditate.

Through this Step, we will become more and more aware of our Higher Power's will for us. We will bring to our conscious mind what the will of our Higher Power is for each one of us individually. We will be listening for that small voice within us that tells us when we're on the right track, or headed the wrong way. We won't try to control how, when or what the message is. We will become more and more willing to follow the will of this force beyond ourselves, because we are starting to see positive results in our lives from doing so.

Many of us were unable before now to maintain any type of change we tried to make. We'd lose 50 pounds, only to gain it back and more. We'd "put the plug in the jug," then two days later take it out again. We'd solemnly resolve to get to work on time each and every day, but within a week we'd be back to showing up late. Using prayer and meditation to stay in conscious contact with our Higher Power will help us to make these changes permanent. We will find the strength and courage we lacked before and we will start to change. We will continue our growth through working with our Higher Power instead of battling and struggling on our own.

When we use prayer and meditation, we develop a better understanding of what works for us, which way we should go or what decision to make. We work at figuring out what is our Higher Power's will and what is our will. Sometimes we might have to discuss our insights with others before we act, especially when we first begin this practice, so we don't just leap into action based on our own subconscious desires.

As we work through these Steps, we get better at knowing when we're acting properly, and when we need to head in another direction. We ask for the strength to lead our lives according to our Higher Power's will. We don't demand that a blueprint be unfolded so we can know and understand everything, instead we trust in our Higher Power and learn to live one day at a time. We have not come this far to fall back to the bottom of the pit we just climbed out of.

There will be times when we ask for guidance from our Higher Power, and we don't get an answer right away. If we feel like we haven't been shown the way to go, that's okay, we stay with that feeling. There are times when to do nothing is better than to charge into action and maybe cause more problems than we had to begin with. Just waiting can be very difficult to do. Many of us want to fix things, or take action, or *do something,* even though we aren't sure what it is we want to do. At such times, we may just need to *be.* Just *being* can be so much more difficult than *doing.* Being sad, being uncomfortable, being angry—these can be awful when we want to rage at someone for what they did, or do something to make us feel happy—even if it's the fleeting happiness a dysfunction like drinking might give us.

Those of us who are self-mutilators may find *being* extremely difficult. After all, we have used pain as a yardstick for measuring our aliveness. We have now learned that we can pray for the understanding to help us overcome this destructive coping mechanism. Our Higher Power helps us see that our bodies belong to no one but us. We accept that we are spiritual beings who have the right and need to live life to its fullest potential.

A lot of us are convinced that we ought to be happy at all times. The media give us that idea; people who care for us give us that idea; books and movies present being happy as the natural way to be. "Don't worry, be happy" is beamed at us from all angles. But the reality is that no one is happy all the time, just as no one is sad all the time, or angry all the time. Nobody is anything *all the time*. Moods pass, situations change, people move on.

> **Reggie shared:** One of the hardest things I had to give up in recovery was the attitude that I had to have excitement all the time in my life. To compensate for my misery when I was being abused, I became a real pleasure seeker—I wanted highs in my life all the time. I have come to accept that I don't need those highs anymore, that peace and serenity are enough.

We must trust that our Higher Power will direct our lives the way they are supposed to go. We let that happen, by asking for guidance and listening for answers. We might get a feeling that one way to act is better than another. We might be chatting with someone who suddenly says exactly what we need to hear. We don't need a tap on the shoulder, our Higher Power can just whisper and we hear the message meant for us and us alone. We might actually hear a voice in our heads telling us what we need to know. Or we may not hear any voice at all. However the answer comes to us, we will be able to act on it because we've been listening and we've been open to our Higher Power's guidance.

We have created a new relationship with our Higher Power; now we will be building on that relationship. Our emotional lives, our souls, need nourishment just as our bodies do, and this drawing closer to our Higher Power provides the spiritual nourishment we need. We will persevere in our efforts to keep getting better, and drawing closer to our Higher Power will be vital. In Step Four, we cleaned out all the garbage and residue from our past, now we are bringing growth into our lives.

When we pray, we don't ask for specific results. We don't ask for our Higher Power to find us a parking space, or to send us a million dollars, or to do anything at all. Prayer is not reciting a wish list as if our Higher Power were Santa Claus. Our Higher Power is not going to reach out a hand and give us whatever we want. When we stop making demands, we start getting help.

> **Sandy began praying every morning, and her prayer was just this simple:** "Dear God, please give me courage today, and help me to be peaceful. Thank you."

Many of us begin our day with prayer. We ask for knowledge of our Higher Power's will for us for the day, and the strength and courage to carry that out. We look ahead to what the day may hold for us. If there are any potentially difficult situations coming up, we ask for special help to deal with any problems that arise. We ask our Higher Power to walk by our side as a special, personal friend. We get a general idea of what our day will be like, and ask for strength to help us through the day.

During the day, we continue to ask for help as we need it. When we are feeling stressed, we take a moment to ask for peace. If we come up against a really tough problem where we seem to be hopelessly stuck, we can repeat a prayer or a phrase that makes us feel closer to our Higher Power until we are calm again. When we need to make a decision and feel confused about what to do, we take a moment to ask for help. We won't get a phone call from our Higher Power, but we may find a moment of peace, and sometimes that's all we really need to figure out what we need to do.

> **Beth said:** When I'm not sure if something is right for me, I ask myself what my Higher Power would do. I know that sounds silly, but for me it works. Somehow I can't imagine my Higher Power stealing, or lying to the boss, or whatever it might be, and that helps me to make better choices.

At night, when we review our day for our Tenth-Step Inventory, we take time out to thank our Higher Power for what we were given that day, and to ask forgiveness for our mistakes. We may need to pray for the strength to make any amends that we owe from that day. We decide how we can do things better the next time, and ask for help to keep growing.

Two prayers that many of us in different Twelve-Step programs have found helpful are the Serenity Prayer and the Prayer of St. Francis. We don't ask for results or concrete things, we ask for wisdom, courage, understanding, etc.

Meditation can be done any time of day. Many of us like to meditate, along with saying our morning prayers, in the early hours before our day begins. Others prefer to do it at night in a quiet time after everyone else has gone to bed. This time is intended only for prayer and meditation. We give ourselves permission to set aside the time necessary to do this daily. As with so many things in this program, it doesn't really matter how or when, the important thing is to do it.

Meditation helps us to calm ourselves, to listen for our Higher Power's guidance. It helps us to see where we're headed, and to feel at peace about where we've been. There are many books and audiocassettes that describe different methods for meditation, or we can create our own meditation. Each of us needs to find what works best in our lives. Some people have time to spend an hour meditating, others might only have 10 minutes. However much time we devote to it, meditation is very important to our recovery.

> **Mary said:** I used to say I didn't have time for that nonsense. My sponsor talked me into trying it for awhile, and now I even get up earlier when necessary to fit it in before I leave for work. I found that I got so many benefits from meditating that it was worth losing a little sleep.

After we have been praying and meditating for awhile, we become aware of possible solutions to our problems and concerns. Some may seem like direct responses, others might come to us over a prolonged period of time. Sometimes, we won't like what the answer seems to be. At times we may think we are asking for our Higher Power's will, when we are really looking for approval from our Higher Power to do things our own way. At such times, we have to be cautious about what interpretations we put on our perceived answers. This is another situation we might want to discuss with a sponsor or other trusted friend. At all times, we must continue to work at distinguishing between what we want and what our Higher Power wants for us, particularly when it comes to what we think others should be doing.

We frequently feel sure we know what would be best for others, if they'd only do things our way, but we must remember that we can't know what would be best for someone else. Even when we have the best interests of a loved one in mind, we can't know what they truly need. They must be allowed to grow on their own, not to our specifications.

> **Sally said:** When I finished going through the Steps the first time, I was so excited that I wanted everyone to have what I had discovered. I went around pushing this person, and urging that one, until I almost drove my friends crazy.

As we continue with our recovery, we will find that prayer and meditation become vital to our spiritual and emotional well-being. It becomes easier to do, almost automatic, because we have begun to see the positive results that come from living a spiritual life.

There may be times when it seems that we just can't say another prayer, or we feel sick at the very thought of meditating again. We may start believing that we have the problem licked, that we're okay now and everything is fine. We have to guard against this attitude. We need to continue our spiritual growth; all the rest—emotional and physical recovery—flows directly from our spiritual well-being. When it is on hold, our whole life is on hold.

Through daily, conscious contact with our Higher Power, we learn to trust ourselves, and our intuition. We realize that, more and more frequently, we are making healthy choices. We reap the benefits of a life filled with peace of mind, wisdom and strength. We realize that we are not alone anymore. Our Higher Power is guiding us with love and gentleness we never knew was possible or never felt we deserved.

Step Eleven Questions

▸ Do you understand the difference between prayer and meditation?

▸ Have you set aside a specific time for your prayer and meditation?

▸ When you need help throughout the day, do you ask your Higher Power for whatever you need?

▸ Have you explored various types of prayer and meditation to find what works for you?

▸ Have you asked other people how they pray or meditate?

▸ Have you looked for books that could help you get comfortable with prayer or meditation?

▸ Have you made the commitment to find a quiet time and place to meditate?

▸ Do you believe that meditation time is healing time?

▸ Do you believe that being quiet and listening is being good to yourself?

▸ Are you able to talk openly with your Higher Power the same way you would with your best friend?

▸ Have you thought about what "conscious contact with a Higher Power" means to you?

▸ Since you started your personal journey of recovery, has your definition and understanding of a Higher Power changed? If so, how?

▸ Have you developed an understanding that works for you?

▸ Are you looking for and seeing signs that could only come from a force beyond yourself?

▸ Does your Higher Power use other people to answer some of your questions?

▸ Do you hear a small voice inside you when you ask for guidance?

▸ Can you accept the answers you get, even when they are not what you want to hear?

▸ If you don't seem to get an answer right away, are you able to wait patiently for guidance?

▸ Are you willing to take whatever action is necessary and then leave the results up to your Higher Power?

▸ Can you believe that your Higher Power is giving you the power, strength and knowledge to do what is right for you today?

▸ Based on today's reality, do the answers feel right?

▸ Can you believe that this force beyond yourself wants only what is good and healing for you?

▸ Using the guidance you receive from your Higher Power, can you continue the changes you have been making in your life?

▸ As you make changes in your life, can you see the ways in which your Higher Power is helping?

▶ Do you believe that you deserve help and guidance from a Higher Power?

▶ Do you feel yourself growing in strength and confidence?

▶ Are you finding life easier now that you have a Higher Power to lend strength and guidance?

▶ Are you seeking knowledge and strength every day from your Higher Power?

▶ Have you given up asking your Higher Power to fill your personal wish list?

▶ Are you finding that peace and serenity fill you up far more than those elusive *highs* you sought before?

▶ Are you asking your Higher Power for courage, wisdom, and freedom from fear?

▶ Are you asking your Higher Power to relieve you of shame and guilt?

▶ Are you guarding against complacency—that feeling that you've got the problem licked and don't need help anymore?

▶ Are you beginning to trust yourself more?

▶ Are you beginning to trust your Higher Power more?

NOTES

Step Twelve

*Having had a spiritual awakening as the result of these
Steps, we tried to carry this message to sexual abuse
survivors, and to practice these principles
in all our affairs.*

Step Twelve

Step Twelve is the last Step in our journey of recovery; the last one, that is, until we begin again—as we will all through our lives. It is perhaps the most challenging Step because it asks us to share our story and our recovery with others, and to continue growing and using these principles throughout our lives. It is the grand culmination, and the ultimate challenge.

This Step first talks about our having a *spiritual awakening*. This simply means a change of attitude regarding how we feel about ourselves and how we see ourselves in the world. Are we still victims, or do we now know that we have rights? We do have rights: the right to be whole and complete; the right to our bodies; the right to our feelings; the right to make our own mistakes. Our imperfection in any of these areas only confirms that we are all imperfect human beings—no better, but certainly no worse, than most other imperfect human beings.

This spiritual awakening also refers to the change in personality that we have experienced as the result of working through these Twelve Steps. As our personalities change, we are more able to deal with our lives and our problems than we ever believed was possible. We rely on our Higher Power more and more as our experiences begin to demonstrate the effectiveness of turning our wills and our lives over to the higher power of our understanding. We become less willing to let anyone violate our new boundaries. We become more able to take control of our lives, to make decisions, and to participate in living, instead of just being observers.

Our change in personality, our "spiritual awakening" and our new attitudes and outlook on life lead to our dependence on a Higher Power from which we get strength and courage. We see the results in our lives of depending on our personal Higher Power, and we have spiritual experiences when we suddenly realize that we are behaving differently in provocative situations, without even thinking about it or straining to control ourselves. Suddenly, or so it seems, we are changed people.

> **Francine, whose mother had abused her for years, related an experience she had early in her recovery process:** I was working in the office of my son's school when a woman that I absolutely detested, because she reminded me of my mother so much, came in to pick up her child. Without realizing what I was doing, I smiled and chatted with her; I even complimented her new haircut. When she left, I went on with my work without giving it a thought. About four hours later, it suddenly hit me that I had reacted to her like I would to anyone—that I had been calm and pleasant, without any sweaty palms or pounding heart. I was astounded, and extremely excited and pleased.

Spiritual experiences can be big or little, burning bushes or little taps on the shoulder. We don't always realize when one has occurred. Sometimes it takes other people mentioning it to us before we realize we've changed. It can be as simple as letting the other person into our lane on the expressway, or it can be as difficult as deciding to make contact with—or confront—our abusers. As we continue to work on our recovery, as we continue to examine our lives and make amends when necessary, when we stand up for ourselves and our rights, our spirituality grows and our peace and serenity blossom.

Many of us used to depend on other people to tell us who we were and how we should feel about anything and everything. Or we went to the other extreme and tried to control everyone and everything around us, telling them how to feel and what to do. We were either overdependent or domineering. All of that is beginning to change as we continue our recovery through the Twelve Steps. We no longer need to cling stubbornly to dependence on other people and stay in our craziness. We now have a Higher Power that we can call on at any time, for any reason. We don't have to dominate or control because we know we will be safe with our Higher Power no matter what anyone else does. We can begin to think for ourselves and trust ourselves because we are relying on a force beyond ourselves now, not on other people who might hurt us.

As much as they might have wanted not to, or as much as we might have wanted others not to, it seemed like sooner or later everyone in our lives let us down. We felt betrayed on all sides, and became less and less willing to trust or to take risks. Other people are just as fallible as we are. We don't have to depend on them anymore—to affirm us or to be manipulated by us. We can let other people be themselves, make their own mistakes and have their own lives, and we can permit ourselves the same thing.

We can get well, and find healing and strength, regardless of what is going on in our lives. No matter who or what tries to destroy us—whether it is someone in our lives right now, or the memories that still haunt us from our past—we can heal and recover. The main things we have to do are to trust our Higher Power with our entire lives and continue our work of cleaning up our lives. We accept responsibility for our actions—making amends when necessary and standing fast when that is appropriate.

As our dependence on or dominance of other people will lessen, our fear of change will lessen, also. When circumstances in our lives aren't what we expect, or when disaster strikes, we will be able to survive and to learn from the experience. There might be times when we again ask our Higher Power: "Why did this happen to me?" or "Where were you when I needed you?" These are the times we need most to remember that our Higher Power does truly love us and will give us the necessary strength to go on. We remember that recovered people are not *cured* forever and we don't have a guarantee that we'll have perfect, trouble-free lives. What we have now is a wonderful method of coping when calamity strikes.

> **Amanda, who had been attacked by several boys in her neighborhood, told us that her daughter died after Amanda had been in a Twelve-Step program for several years. She felt devastated. She clung to her Higher Power and to the people in her program, who were able to be there for her and to support her when she most needed it:** I would never have survived that experience and stayed sane if it hadn't been for the love and support I received from my group. And even though my faith in God faltered, deep down inside, I know the main reason I'm here today is God's love and help, and the love of my friends. My friends in the program loved and helped me until I was strong enough to love and help myself.

Sometimes people think that they don't need all twelve Steps—that things are going along just fine with only doing Steps One, Two and Three, or with only Steps One and Twelve. Or sometimes we get complacent and think that, since life is rolling along fine, and we don't have any major problems anymore, we don't need to continue to grow. These are very dangerous attitudes to fall into.

It's like building a deck with twelve strong pillars to support it, then one of the pillars gets knocked down for some reason. The deck still seems strong, so we go along with just eleven pillars. Then another couple of pillars fall. The deck is getting a little wobbly, but it still serves its purpose, so we still don't do anything about it. Pretty soon, a storm breaks, lightning strikes, and the deck collapses. We're left tumbled down among the wreckage, wondering what happened.

The recovery we get from our efforts on the Twelve Steps is just like the deck. We need to continually maintain it and strengthen it with our work and energy. It is only too true that we get back just exactly as much as we put in. If we put in a little effort, we only get little results. When we work hard and put in a lot of effort, then we get wonderful results.

We build our base, our deck, and we keep it well-maintained for those times when catastrophe hits, or when we feel overwhelmed by our memories, or when flashbacks occur. Things will happen, good and bad, and this program will prepare us to handle what life brings us. We'll be able to accept and solve our problems instead of running from them or feeling hopeless and overwhelmed by them. We have lessened our expectations and learned to accept what happens. We don't need to change others, control others, or overdepend on others any longer.

The middle part of this Step says that we "try to carry this message" to survivors of sexual abuse and incest. It's important to see and understand the word *try* in this Step. It means we make an effort. There will be people who don't want to hear us, or who can't hear us because of where they are in their lives. It will be tempting to want to save the world; it's natural to want to share this gift with everyone we meet. There will be times when we fall into preaching to others, rather than sharing with them. These are some of the mistakes we need to avoid as we try to carry the message.

There are many different ways to carry the message. Members of Twelve-Step groups already have a fellowship around them with whom they can share their recovery. Perhaps those in group or individual therapy can share this message. If there are no Twelve-Step groups in the area, we can start one (addresses for further information are listed in the Appendix). We can contact hospitals, clinics and therapists in our area for more information. Most states have a self-help clearinghouse, usually an 800 number, that should have information about groups we can join. We can talk to the people with whom we feel safe about how we have been able to work through our own problems regarding sexual abuse. We discuss how incest and sexual abuse controlled our lives, and how we are now in control of our feelings and reactions. We share how we have used the healing tools we have gained through our personal journey of recovery.

The important thing about carrying this message is that each of us is a living example of how well this program works. When we are living these Steps to the best of our ability, we serve as models for others, showing them the possibilities that are attainable through the recovery process. We demonstrate daily how we focus on ourselves as we are today, and leave our yesterdays behind as problems that we have overcome. We have moved the pain from the inside to the outside, and have forgiven ourselves for the hurts we have carried around within us and acted out on others. We have replaced the toxic shame that almost ruined us with the healthy embarrassment that tells us we've been wrong.

When we are living in health and serenity, it shines out of us.

Toni, who was abused by her uncle for many years, told us that even the people at work noticed something different: They kept asking me if I'd lost weight, or had a new hair style, or what was going on. They could tell something had changed, but weren't sure what. My secretary said that I sort of gleamed. I knew I was glowing with my deep peace and happiness.

When we talk with someone who is a survivor of sexual abuse or incest, we share our story with them. We tell them a little bit about what happened to us, and the effects the abuse had on our lives. This doesn't have to be morbid and depressing. We let the other person dictate the mood of our discussion. If they are hurting badly and feeling very depressed, the last thing they need to hear is how miserable our lives were. We don't want to get into "if you think you had it bad, let me tell you ..." That type of attitude helps no one. We discuss some of the problems and attitudes we developed as survivors of abuse—perhaps our lack of trust in others, or fear of new situations, or how we spent our days worrying about what would happen or had happened.

> **Alicia, who was forced to participate in child pornography, shares with newcomers why she was overweight for so long:** I used the eighty pounds of fat that I carried around as a defense against any more abuse and to deny myself as being a female. It was eighty pounds of grief, sadness and defense mechanism to keep people away from me so I would not be hurt again. I am now in control of myself and my life. I am a recovering woman who will not stop recovering as long as I continue to put the focus on myself and keep my power in my control. People who knew me a year ago ask me what happened, and I am glad to answer that I am dealing daily with my core issue of having been abused as a child.

We are not there to preach at anyone or make anyone think they have any obligation to do anything at all. We are there to share our experience, strength and hope, without any expectation of a reward or that the person will change anything. We simply let them know that what we are doing is helping us to recover far more than anything else we try. We offer friendship, acceptance and belief; we make no demands on them. When we work with others, we get out of our own "stuff," and focus on another's life, which helps us to see our own life in a new perspective.

> **Leona, abused for years by her next-door neighbor, shared that sometimes she forgets what has changed in her own life until she talks with a newcomer:** I'll share how I've changed, and offer examples of what improvements they might expect in their lives, and suddenly I realize that it's been months since I did exactly what I'm talking about. It surprises me, but it's also fun to see in concrete ways exactly how I'm changing.

When we talk with someone for the first time, we don't push our program on them. If they don't want to hear about it, then we let it be, knowing that we've planted a seed that might or might not germinate. We are not responsible for anyone else's recovery. They have to decide for themselves if they want what we have to offer. We are only responsible for our lives and our own recovery. We think about how we would want someone to talk to us if we were the newcomer, and we remember to take things slowly. We stay focused on our experience, and remain non-judgmental about them.

We talk freely about the fact that this is a spiritual program. We stress, however, that no particular religion is the *right* answer. Even though we might have a strong belief in our own religion, we assure the new person they can believe in whatever power they choose. Some people might be resistant to the idea of any higher power at all. We assure them they can still begin this program and that eventually they may discover for themselves a Higher Power they can trust. The main things they will need are a belief in their own personal force beyond themselves and a willingness to live by the spiritual principles they will soon learn.

If the thought of writing an inventory or making amends turns them off, we reassure them that they don't have to do everything right away; that when the time comes, they will be ready because they will have done the work that leads up to each Step.

One of the most important things we can do for someone new to this program is to listen to them. We listen to their story—if they want to share some of it—and we hear their pain. We assure them that we believe their story, and we are willing to listen to what they have to say and accept it unconditionally and non-judgmentally. We will be unable to help some people, for whatever reason, and others will need professional help as well as the fellowship of the program. Professional help is always warranted if someone is feeling self-destructive.

Once we are working with someone, as a sponsor or a friend-in-recovery, we remember that we are not responsible for their actions or reactions. We don't want to smother them with help or encourage them to wallow in their situation. Sometimes what will be needed is a gentle nudge—"have you thought about writing an inventory about that," or "whenever I feel like that, I start praying and meditating, and asking for help." We don't allow ourselves to get wrapped up in their problems as a mediator or a judge. We offer a listening ear, share any similar experiences with them, and encourage them to keep on with their recovery.

> **Patrice frequently shares with newcomers how she was able to stop hating her perpetrators and to see them as human beings who were very hurt themselves. She could see her parents as very sick people who could not hurt her today unless she let them:** I hated their disease and dysfunction but could give them the dignity of their sickness and disease without judging them or trying to change them into the people I wanted them to be. I found functional and healthy people who would and could love me today just as I am, not as what they wanted me to be.

There may be times when we have to end a sponsoring relationship. If the person we are working with is absolutely unresponsive, then we need to release them. If, after many honest efforts to share our recovery, they are determined to remain the same, we turn our efforts to someone else. Discussion with our sponsor or other caring friends will help us to decide if this is a necessary step.

The last part of this Step asks us to try to "practice these principles in all our affairs." This can be the most challenging aspect of all the Steps. We are asked in Step Twelve to take what we have learned through working these Steps and put those principles into practice in every aspect of our lives—not just those concerning our abuse issues, but every single part of our lives. We know that being sexually abused has affected every aspect of our lives. Now we try to use these spiritual principles to help heal every aspect of our lives.

In the first three Steps, we learned self-honesty and awareness, hope and faith. By working Steps Four through Nine, we practiced courage, more honesty, willingness, humility and responsibility. By doing Steps Ten and Eleven every day, we worked with perseverance and deepened our spirituality. In doing Step Twelve, we not only repeat and strengthen these principles, but we add love, openness, unselfishness, acceptance, tolerance, peace of mind and serenity. In addition to these spiritual principles, we learned concrete actions to take: prayer and meditation, writing, talking with others, making amends if necessary, acknowledging our good qualities and actions.

Some of us use the word *HALT* when we can't figure out why we feel bad. It's time to *HALT* if we are too Hungry, Angry, Lonely or Tired, as we are more likely to slip back into old, unhealthy behaviors. This is another effective coping skill we can use to heal our wounds.

This Step says "we tried to practice." We attempt, according to Webster, to do something repeatedly so as to gain skill. We are never going to be perfect at these things. It will probably be more difficult at the beginning of our recovery process. We are learning how to do these things and to take responsibility for our lives, and we will make mistakes, just as all learners do. But it will get easier, like anything does when we keep working at it. When we slip, we repair the damage as soon as possible. When we do things well, we congratulate ourselves. Gradually, over our lifetimes, there will be more congratulations than slips, as long as we keep working on our spiritual growth.

We are working toward unselfish, constructive action. This does not mean that we become people-pleasers. Doing what we think everyone else wants us to do is not helpful—to them or to us. We think about how our actions might affect others, then we decide if our actions would be beneficial to ourselves without hurting anyone else. When we are able to take care of ourselves—to take care of our needs—we will be able to help others.

Sometimes, when we experience the peace and serenity that are possible with this program, and we see how well the Steps work in our lives, we slip into the attitude that we have the answer for everyone. We start finding fault with others if they don't do things the way we think they should. We start believing that our way is so terrific that it must be the right way for everyone, everywhere. We want to heal the world, especially our little corner of it. When we realize this is happening—and sometimes we find out the hard way when someone tells us to "butt out!"—we back off and remember that our way may be the best for us, but not necessarily the best way for others. We live our program to the best of our ability and let our actions exemplify our beliefs. It can be amazing how the people around us change just by watching our progress.

> **Todd was raised in an alcoholic household where no secrets were told and nothing was explained, especially about his father's drinking or his mother's sexual abuse of him:** I never explained to anyone why I did things, and I never apologized. I figured that, if I was wrong—which was very unlikely—then the other person would just

forget about it, or it would all blow over, I didn't need to say anything. After going through the Steps, I realized I couldn't go on like that anymore, and I started making amends when I was in the wrong. I even apologized to my children when necessary. I got the shock of my life, and a very warm feeling, when I overheard my eight-year-old son apologizing, without any pressure from anyone, to his sister for something he had done to her. That certainly never would have happened before my recovery.

The benefits of working this Step are enormous. We are continually reinforcing our new habits and attitudes. We are helping others in a healthy way. We are peaceful and serene, most of the time. We can handle anything that comes our way because we have a powerful support system—our Higher Power, the Steps, and our network of recovering people. As we continue to work on our spiritual growth, the other aspects of our lives fall into place without much effort.

As we stay centered in recovery, our relationships with everyone around us become healthier. We are able to see when a relationship is unhealthy and we are able to do something about it. Sometimes a relationship is so unhealthy that it must be eliminated from our lives, or perhaps we just need to have an honest, open discussion of feelings, attitudes and expectations. We will begin to attract healthy people into our lives. We will develop sharing, caring relationships that are balanced partnerships, with an easy, mutual give and take. We will no longer be anyone's slave, or anyone's dictator.

We will get out of our isolation and loneliness. We've hidden behind our walls long enough. Now we can come out and enjoy life. We can release the past, and regain power and control over our own lives. We may not ever be rich or famous, but we will find a deep satisfaction with what we do, no matter what it is.

Step Twelve Questions

▶ Have your thinking, feelings and attitudes begun to change as a result of working through these Steps?

▶ If they have, how do you feel about that?

▶ If you haven't noticed any changes yet, how do you feel about that?

▶ Have other people noticed any changes in you?

▶ What has happened to you as a result of working and living the Twelve Steps?

▶ Thinking back over the past month or the past year, are you the same person, or have there been subtle changes?

▶ Do you feel that your life is more manageable?

▶ Did you expect more differences than have appeared?

▶ Do you feel you're finished and won't ever have to do anything like this again, or do you believe that these Steps are a guide, to be used daily in your continuing recovery?

▶ Have you found yourself not doing or saying something so you would not have to make amends to someone?

▶ Have you found yourself using old coping skills, then suddenly remembering you have new techniques for dealing with problems?

▶ Have you found yourself instinctively seeking guidance and help from your Higher Power?

▶ Have you dropped the barriers you had put up to protect yourself from other people?

▶ Are you finding it easier to cope with daily life?

▶ Are you able to stay in today's reality more than you were before these Steps?

▶ Can you make decisions more easily?

▶ Are you better able to stand up for your rights and assert yourself, when necessary?

▸ Is your life becoming an example of what happens when someone strives for recovery?

▸ Are you willing to talk with other survivors about what happened in your life and how things have changed?

▸ If the people you talk with are unable to hear your message, do you separate with love so you can help someone who can hear your message?

▸ When you share with someone, are you doing so with no expectations that they will do anything at all?

▸ Can you share your story with others without preaching?

▸ When you share with others, are you listening impartially, or are you jumping into their problems, trying to solve them all?

▸ Are these Twelve Steps a guide for recovery and change in every aspect of your life?

▸ Are you remembering to take it one step at a time?

▸ Are you willing to keep practicing the principles you have learned, to continue writing, praying and meditating, and continue making amends where necessary?

▸ Are you willing to examine your positive aspects and give yourself full credit for them?

▸ Are you willing to be proud of yourself when you are acting in a healthy manner?

▸ Are you reinforcing your new behaviors with positive self-talk and praise?

▸ Are you learning to love yourself unconditionally?

Epilogue

By following the Twelve Steps, we have found a new person inside each one of us. Where once we were broken, we are now whole. Where once we were so unfinished, we are now complete. Where once our inner light was just a flicker, it is now a steady glow, growing bigger and brighter with each passing day. The Twelve Steps helped us to change our attitudes and our thinking. Because our attitudes and our thinking changed, our actions and reactions have also changed. We became aware of the old habits and coping skills that no longer worked for us. We began to change them; to replace them with healthy new ways of coping. We didn't forget about the abuse we suffered, and we didn't necessarily forgive the people who abused us. We decided it was time to put down our burden of hatred and resentment and to set ourselves free to soar as we were always meant to, but weren't allowed to before. The results we got from working these Steps were incredible. There was a dramatic change in our thinking and attitudes. We began to react differently than we did prior to going through this process. We have not been *cured;*we are stronger, healthier, more healed. We continue to work this program of recovery. We keep watching for our old habits to creep back into our lives, as they will if we aren't careful. This is a program of awareness, and as long as we continue to be aware, we can continue our healing.

Worry and fear have lessened their grip on our lives. We still have moments of indecision and worry, but they are few and far between. There are times when we feel fearful, perhaps when something happens that reminds us of being abused, but now we call on our Higher Power to give us courage, and we assure ourselves and our inside kids that we are safe—we wrap ourselves in the love of our Higher Power and know that we are secure, centered, and grounded in today's reality.

We aim for a balanced life in all areas of our lives: relationships, work, money, food, sex, etc. Where we used to live at the extremes—wildly excited or deeply depressed, brave enough to conquer the world or too afraid to leave our homes—now we realize that we don't need those highs and lows anymore. We have experienced the balance of life on a middle ground, filled with calm and peace, and that is excitement enough for our lives.

> **Natalie shared her feelings about this:** I thought the middle ground was the way I felt most of my life—life was gray, I was a blob and the world generally was yucky. Now I realize that was depression and that I don't feel that way anymore. Life in the middle is bright and cheerful, a complete rainbow of colors, with many days of happiness interspersed with a few moments of unrest.

We are content with life, with whatever comes our way. We don't react with childishness or grandiosity any longer. We are no longer oversensitive to everyone else's opinions. We understand that they have their ideas—about us and about life in general—and they have the right to their ideas. We also have the right to our ideas and ideals. We have become individuals, no longer enmeshed in others' lives.

Our self-esteem is centered on us and our beliefs about ourselves, not on power over others or others' opinions of us. We know and finally accept that we are good people, that what was done to us was not our fault. The abusers and perpetrators were the ones who were wrong when they used us. We are not bad people.

We are building pride in ourselves. Our self-esteem, of which we had little or none before, is growing. We like ourselves now, and are adjusting to what our hopes and dreams are. We don't have to please others—we can be ourselves, instead of chameleons reflecting the attitudes of those around us. We are growing and becoming the people we were meant to be.

Each of us has worked hard, and for some of us it's been many years, to get to this place in our lives. Our journey has not been an easy one—many of us have stumbled and fallen, only to pick ourselves up and start all over again. We have chosen a new life. We won't let anyone steal our personal healing. It was earned by each of us, and is ours to keep and to protect for the rest of our lives.

Is this the end? *No!* We have found this new freedom and happiness, and now we must work daily to keep it. Sometimes we'll get tired and weary, but we must hold on. It will all be worth it.

We—Pat and Jean—hope that each of you have found a new you, just as we have found ourselves by sharing our experience, strength and hope with you.

God bless you all.

Resource List

This list of organizations is provided to enhance your recovery. The authors do not endorse any of the organizations; this is simply an effort to make you aware of some of the resources available to survivors of sexual abuse and incest. These resources are not listed in any particular order.

Organizations Specific to Sexual Abuse

> Sexual Abuse Survivors Anonymous (S.A.S.A.)
> World Service Headquarters
> P.O. Box 241046
> Detroit, MI 48224
> (313) 882-9646

A Twelve Step self-help group of female and male survivors who are recovering and learning to live in today's reality.

> Survivors of Incest Anonymous (S.I.A.)
> World Service Office
> P.O. Box 21817
> Baltimore, MD 21222-2365
> (410) 433-2365

A self-help group of adult men and women based on the Twelve Steps of Alcoholics Anonymous model. International groups, bimonthly bulletins, pen pals. We define incest very broadly. For further information, please send a self-addressed stamped envelope.

> VOICES In Action, Inc. (Victims of Incest Can Emerge Survivors)
> P.O. Box 148309
> Chicago, IL 60614
> (312) 327-1500 or (800) 7-VOICE-8

Survivors and pro-survivors dedicated to prevention and recovery through networking, support and education.

One of Many Voices
1275 Fourth St., #231
Santa Rosa, CA 95404

A non-profit organization for those who have PTSD (Post Traumatic Stress Disorder) due to childhood sexual abuse.

W.I.N.G.S. Foundation, Inc. (Women Incested Needing Group Support)
8007 West Colfax Ave.
C.S. #27 Box 129
Lakewood, CO 80215
(303) 238-8660 (day)

Promotes healing through support groups to reduce the trauma of incest. Addresses issue of isolation. Newsletter, information, conferences, referrals to therapists and support groups.

Parents United
232 East Gish Road
San Jose, CA 95112
(408) 453-7616 or 453-7611

Guided self-help program (not Twelve Step) for abused children, and adults who were abused as children.

M.A.L.E. (Men Assisting, Leading & Educating)
P.O. Box 380181
Denver, CO 80238-1181
(303) 320-4365

A non-profit organization for non-offending male survivors of child sexual abuse. Provides seminars, workshops, information and referral services, intervention and outreach programs. Also publishes newsletter called "Men's Issues Forum."

National Organization for Victim Assistance (NOVA)
1757 Park Road N.W.
Washington, DC 20010

An organization that assists persons who have been sexually assaulted.

Other Organizations

Alcoholics Anonymous World Services, Inc.
475 Riverside Drive
New York, NY 10115
(212) 870-3400

Alcoholics Anonymous is a program of recovery from alcoholism.

Al-Anon Family Groups, Inc.
P.O. Box 862
Midtown Station
New York, NY 10018-0862
(212) 302-7240

For families and friends of alcoholics.

Overeaters Anonymous World Service Office
383 Van Ness, Suite. 1601
Torrance, CA 90501
(310) 618-8835
For meeting listings only: (800) 743-8703

A fellowship of individuals who, through shared experience, strength and hope, are recovering from compulsive overeating. "We welcome everyone who wants to stop eating compulsively."

Debtors Anonymous
P.O. Box 400
New York, NY 10163-0400

A fellowship of men and women who share their experience, strength and hope in combating their common problem of compulsive indebtedness.

Gamblers Anonymous
P.O. Box 17173
Los Angeles, CA 90017

A support group for people fighting compulsive gambling.

Sexaholics Anonymous
P.O. Box 300
Simi Valley, CA 93062
(805) 581-3343

A program of recovery for those who want to stop their sexually self-destructive thinking and behavior.

Emotions Anonymous
P.O. Box 4245
St. Paul, MN 55104

For emotional health through the Twelve Steps.

Multiple Personality Dignity/Loved Ones of Multiples
P.O. Box 4367
Boulder, CO 80306-4367

International; non-religious twelve-practices; newsletter, chapters, pen/phone pals. Include self-addressed stamped envelope for details.

National Association for Children of Alcoholics
11426 Rockville Pike, Suite 100
Rockville, MD 20852
(301) 468-0985

An association for children of alcoholics—of all ages—who have been impacted by alcoholism or other drug abuse.

Recovery, Inc.
802 North Dearborn Street
Chicago, IL 60610

Community mental health organization that offers systematic training in a self-help method of controlling temperamental behavior and handling anxiety, depression and fears at weekly group meetings for persons aged 18 or over. No fee is required; a free-will offering is collected at the conclusion of each meeting.

Co-Dependents Anonymous, Inc.
P.O. Box 33577
Phoenix, AZ 85067-3577
(602) 277-7991

A self-help group organized to assist people caught up in the dysfunction of loved ones.

Resources

American Self-Help Clearinghouse
St. Clares-Riverside Medical Center
Denville, NJ 07834
(201) 625-7101

Provides phone information on national self-help groups for abuse, addictions, disabilities, bereavement, illnesses and other stressful problems. Publishes directory.

ChildHelp USA
Adult Survivors Program
1345 El Centro Avenue
P.O. Box 630
Hollywood, CA 90028
800-4-A-CHILD

A professionally staffed crisis line, referral service and resource for anyone concerned about child abuse.

The National Resource Center on Child Sexual Abuse
107 Lincoln Street
Huntsville, AL 35801
800-543-7006

Interesting publications on child abuse and recovery are available.

Button and Dietz, Inc.
Human Resources Consultants
P.O. Box 19243
Austin, TX 78760-9243

Supplies free copy of a survivors reading list and resource list. Also holds intensive workshops for sexual abuse survivors and partners in intimate relationships.

SASAM, Inc.
P.O. Box 884
Keller, TX 76248
800-25-SASAM (800-257-2726)

Works with males 18 years and older who are survivors of sexual abuse and rape.

Above and Beyond
P.O. Box 2672
Ann Arbor, MI 48106-2672
800-821-5341

Excellent resource of books, tapes and information on healing resources and survivors issues. Good resource for male survivors.

Incest Survivors Resource Network International (ISRNI)
P.O. Box 7375
Las Cruces, NM 88006-7375
(505) 521-4260

A Quaker witness educational resource ... mainly by participation in committees of international organizations.

SURVIVORSHIP
3181 Mission Street, #139
San Francisco, CA 94110

A forum on survival of ritual abuse, torture and mind control.

SOUNDINGS
Echoes Network Counseling Center, Inc.
1622 N.E. 8th
Portland, OR 97232
(503) 281-8185

A newsletter for survivors of childhood sexual abuse; a non-profit counseling center.

SURVIVOR
P.O. Box 11315
Knoxville, TN 37939-1315
(615) 637-0869

A bi-monthly creative journal by men and women survivors of sexual assault.

Above a Whisper
P.O. Box 2588
Ann Arbor, MI 48106-2588
(313) 572-9308

A newsletter written by and for women survivors of incest/childhood sexual abuse.

Many Voices
P.O. Box 2639
Cincinnati, OH 45201-2639

A national bi-monthly self-help publication for persons with multiple personalities, or a dissociative disorder, and their therapists.

Incest Survivor Information Exchange (ISIE)
P.O. Box 3399
New Haven, CT 06515

A national, non-profit newsletter published by female survivors. "Our purpose is to provide a forum for men and women who have survived incest to publish their thoughts, writings and art work and to exchange information."

Stand Fast
P.O. Box 9107
Warwick, RI 02889
(401) 737-7505 (Voice/TDD)

A networking/newsletter for non-perpetrating partners of adult survivors of sexual abuse, ritual or cult abuse, and multiple personalities.

MPD REACHING OUT
c/o Public Relations Department
Royal Ottawa Hospital
1145 Carling Ave.
Ottawa, Ontario, Canada K1Z 7K4

A newsletter about Multiple Personality Disorder.

National Victim Center
309 West Seventh Street, Suite 705
Fort Worth, TX 76102

An assistance center helping victims nationwide.

Healing Hearts Project/Bay Area Women Against Rape
357 MacArthur Blvd.
Oakland, CA 94610

Information and referral for survivors of ritual abuse; conducts annual survivor conferences.

NOW Legal Defense and Education Fund
99 Hudson Street
New York, NY 10013

Distributes legal resource kit for adult survivors of incest and child sexual abuse, including attorney directory. Other written material available includes information on statutes of limitations, bibliographies and model legal documents. Provides technical assistance to attorneys, legislators and others on extending the statute of limitations through legislation and litigation.

Other Family Problem-Solving Books
... From Mills & Sanderson, Publishers

Pulling Together: Crisis Prevention for Teens and Their Parents, by Dr. Harold D. Jester, with a foreword by Jacob Roseman, M.D. A veteran family counselor offers easy-to-follow advice to help teens and their parents learn to get along together and appreciate each other's good points. $9.95

The Big Squeeze: Balancing the Needs of Aging Parents, Dependent Children, and YOU, by Barbara A. Shapiro, Ph.D., with Vicki Konover and Ann Shapiro. An 8-step survival plan for dealing with the simultaneous needs of the three generations. $12.95

Better Bodies After 35: A Commonsense Approach to Healthful Living, by Irving A. Beychok, M.D. A down-to-earth guide to staying or getting fit once you have matured beyond the need to perfect your body as a means of impressing others. A great aide for all those people interested in good health, from age 35 to 135. $9.95

The Suddenly Single Mother's Survival Guide, by L. Patricia Kite. A modern-day guide to life after hubby, this delightful guide is both informative and honest, offering advice on all that ails the single-again mother. $9.95

The 50 Healthiest Places to Live and Retire in the United States, by Norman D. Ford. Detailed breakdowns on what makes these 50 top ranked cities the healthiest locals in which to make your home. $12.95

Childbirth Choices in Mothers' Words, by Kim Selbert, M.F.C.C., with a foreword by noted childbirth author Carl Jones. These personal stories offer expectant parents a look at the various birthing options currently available in the United States. $9.95

60-Second Shiatzu: How to Energize, Erase Pain, and Conquer Tension in One Minute, by Eva Shaw. A helpfully illustrated, quick-results introduction to do-it-yourself acupressure. $8.95

We gladly accept consumer orders by telephone. Just call 800-441-6224 and ask us to bill you with shipment. If you prefer, complete the order form on the next page and return it to us with full payment.

Order Form

If you are unable to find our books in your local bookstore, you may order them directly from us. Simply note the book(s) you're ordering and enclose check or money order for the amount of your purchase plus a handling charge of $1.50 per book.

( ) Jester, *Pulling Together* $9.95

( ) Shapiro/Konover/Shapiro, *The Big Squeeze* $12.95

( ) Beychok, *Better Bodies After 35* $9.95

( ) Kite, *The Suddenly Single Mother's Survival Guide* $9.95

( ) Ford, *The 50 Healthiest Places to Live and Retire* $12.95

( ) Selbert, *Childbirth Choices in Mothers' Words* $9.95

( ) Shaw, *60-Second Shiatzu* $8.95

$1.50 handling charge per book

5% sales tax for MA residents

Total amount enclosed

Name: _____

Address: _____

City: _____ State: _____ Zip code: _____ – _____

( ) Please, send me your complete catalog with my order.

Mail to: Mills & Sanderson, Publishers
41 North Road, Suite 201
Bedford, MA 01730

OR, call our toll free Order Line: 1-800-441-6224.